THE TENNESSEE GRASSROOTS WRITER

THE AMERICAN GRASSROOTS WRITER SERIES

THE TENNESSEE GRASSROOTS WRITER

James A. Crutchfield • Peter S. LaPaglia

HILLSBORO PRESS

Franklin, Tennessee

TENNESSEE HERITAGE LIBRARY
Bicentennial Collection

Printed in the United States of America

00   99   98   97   96   5   4   3   2   1

Library of Congress Card Catalog Number: 96-67477

ISBN: 1-881576-51-5

Cover by Bozeman Design

*Thanks to James B. Gardner for his editorial
assistance and technical advice.*

Published by
HILLSBORO PRESS
an imprint of
PROVIDENCE HOUSE PUBLISHERS
238 Seaboard Lane • Franklin, Tennessee 37067
800-321-5692

To the memory of Bradley Whitfield, who dramatically influenced my early writing career.

—James A. Crutchfield

To my mother, Louise Watson LaPaglia, whose love and support are with me always.

—Peter S. LaPaglia

CONTENTS

Preface
A Special Word to the Reader

Should you already not be keenly interested in history—and just maybe, inspired with the possibility of writing something about some phase of it—you most likely would not be reading these words right now. You're reading this book because, somewhere in the back of your mind—gnawing, gnawing, gnawing—is a deep-seated desire to put important and meaningful words down on paper, words that will be passed along to future generations, words you hope will teach, enlighten, amuse, and educate. Whether your goal is to lionize your great-grandparents, trace the history and development of the family business, document the life and times of your community or county, or just simply to produce a collection of thoughts about growing up in your neck of the woods, you want to write it! But, how, you might ask?

Well, that all-important question, "How?" is what this book is all about. It is the hope of the authors that, when you complete reading its pages, this small volume will have imparted some valuable information that will prove to be useful in your desire to research and to write that important story that you so badly want to tell. Although we don't purport to have ready-made answers for all of the hundreds of unique situations that might be encountered in the course of writing a book, we do believe that we have provided a great deal of common-sense logic and information that will assist a would-be writer in his or her pursuit of local history.

Local history, or what we like to call "grassroots" history, has many outlets. Basically, however, the writing of this brand of history is all, pretty much, alike. With the exception of genealogical research and writing—which incidentally, is not pursued in this volume other than in brief passing—most local histories, regardless of what the subject is, can be pursued in a like manner and produce similar-looking final results.

When you finish reading this book from cover to cover, you might find yourself reflecting upon how simple it all seems. And, it *is* simple. The hard part is getting organized, knowing where to look for what, and the absolute, most difficult phase of all, sitting down at a yellow tablet, typewriter, word processor, or personal computer and doing it!

We all have an obligation to the past to document its varied life and times before it is too late. We owe a debt to the present—in reality tomorrow's past—to see that mechanisms are in place to preserve its wonderful stories and tales and places from eventual loss by a disinterested and apathetic public. But, perhaps, as historians and historical writers, our greatest responsibility is to guarantee tomorrow's unnumbered generations that they will be the recipients of a firm foundation of sound, well-researched history.

WHAT IS LOCAL HISTORY AND WHY WRITE ABOUT IT? 1

W ebster's College Dictionary defines the word "history" as "the record of past events and times." The word "local" in the same dictionary is defined as "pertaining to or characterized by place." Put the two definitions together, and we get an accurate and acceptable definition of local history, i.e., "the record of past events and times in a particular place."

But just because that "particular place" is not a state or nation is no reason to assume that it is not just as important; indeed, the argument can be made that local history is *more* important. When Henry Ford dismissed history as "bunk," according to David E. Kyvig and Myron A. Marty in *Nearby History* (Nashville: American Association for State and Local History Press, 1982),

> He did not believe 'history' had any significance for his everyday life; the word referred, he thought, only to the stories of colonial settlement and early national development, presidential achievement, and military victory which constituted the bulk of

1

historical literature in his day. . . . It was the experiences, the beliefs and behavior, and the changes in the lives of average people over the generations which interested him. Henry Ford was ignorant, even contemptuous, of traditional 'history,' but he instinctively knew that what had happened nearby, to himself, his ancestors, his neighbors, and other ordinary people, had shaped their lives. Events and conditions in his family, church, school, workplace, and community had helped form him and his personal world. To Ford, such nearby history was not 'bunk'; it was very important. (p. 1)

Indeed, the ordinary people and everyday lives of our local communities are as central to understanding our past as the great men and great events that fill the pages of United States history textbooks. It is only through study of the former that we can learn the details, the particulars, the varieties of experiences that add up to form our larger shared experiences, our history as a state or nation.

Nor should the focus on a "particular place" be seen as limiting or restrictive. According to Carol Kammen, author of *On Doing Local History: Reflections on What Local Historians Do, Why, and What It Means* (Nashville: American Association for State and Local History Press, 1986), *local history* is:

. . . a broad field of inquiry: it is the political, social, and economic history of a community, and religious and intellectual history, too. It is a place to look for individual reactions to historical events. . . . Local history is the place to hear

women's voices, find information about child-rear-
ing practices, ask questions related to education,
leisure, and privacy. Local history allows us to look
at town planning and our domestic architecture. It
begs for studies of how we have lived in the past, in
this particular place, and it offers an opportunity to
study group biography, leadership, philanthropy,
crime, and gender. Local history is the study of who
remained in a community and who left—and why.
. . . Local history is, at its heart . . . the study of the
human condition in and through time." (p. 5)

As we as a people become more and more mobile,
local history, according to Kammen, provides us with
"a sense of place and an understanding of continu-
ity." In the early 1970s, author Jim Crutchfield
plunged into the arena of writing local and regional
history. His subject was the Harpeth River, a
medium-sized stream which runs for about 120 miles
in and out of five Middle Tennessee counties before it
enters the Cumberland River downstream from
Nashville. His express purpose in researching and
writing the book was two-fold: First, no book-length
work had ever before been done on the river and its
interesting tributary system, even though the
stream's watershed area encompassed some of
Middle Tennessee's most historic and interesting real
estate. Secondly, he was truly concerned over
whether this precious history could be preserved
before the rapidly spreading growth of nearby
Nashville obliterated all traces of the river's past. Two
decades have now passed since the publication of *The
Harpeth River: A Biography*, and urban sprawl and

too-rapid development have indeed changed the face and complexion of the Harpeth River valley as well as its inhabitants. Only through the words and illustrations of the book will future generations be able to visualize what things were like in the five rural river counties before the rapid expansion of the greater Nashville metropolitan area changed them so dramatically.

The old saying, "We're not getting any younger," has truth in the life of buildings, institutions, and communities just as it does among humans. And, as each and every year passes, we lose just a little bit more of our heritage and history. An old schoolhouse here, a home in the way of progress there, and one of the community's oldest and most knowledgeable citizens in between—they're all passing one by one. Unless we as historians and writers—regardless of our amateur or professional status—make conscientious efforts now to do something about preserving through the written word what we can while we can, it will soon be too late.

WHAT IS LEFT TO WRITE? 2

The two most frequently asked questions—and certainly legitimate ones—that aspiring local history writers ask are simply, "What can I write about?" and "What is left that hasn't already been explored and exploited to the fullest?" There are quick, one-word answers to both inquiries: "Plenty" and "Plenty."

When one tours the local history reading room at one of the large city libraries across Tennessee, or more especially, when he or she enters the sanctuary of the Tennessee State Library and Archives in Nashville (TSL&A), a sense of awe and respect immediately sets in. For the thousands of writers who have labored over the past two hundred years and more to assure that our precious heritage will be preserved, we will forever be grateful. Along with that feeling of respect is an amazement at the sheer quantity of material that has already been produced about some facet of Tennessee history. But there is now, and always will be, room for additional studies in local and regional history.

While planning the contents of this chapter, the authors identified several previously published books that were among our favorites and then further identified several ideas for what we believe to be extremely attractive and potentially marketable books, all of which beg to be well-researched and written. We believe these will serve as examples of what we are saying here. The published ones we'll tell you about should prove to you that we, as local history writers, are not "wed in the woods" to just county histories, or town histories, or corporate histories, or church histories, or family histories, vital and necessary as these types of documentation are. There are larger studies that need addressing as well, studies that still, nevertheless, fall under the category of local history.

One of the finest local history books is entitled *Night Riders of Reelfoot Lake*, by Paul J. Vanderwood (Memphis State University Press, 1969). Taking an event that started out as a purely localized kidnapping/murder in extreme northwestern Tennessee, Vanderwood, with the finesse of Earle Stanley Gardner, wove his tale of tragedy and pathos, and sometimes even humor, into a 159-page, illustrated book that would be difficult for anyone to put down.

Another case in point involves a book written by Tennessee's official state historian, Wilma Dykeman. In 1978, Dykeman and her son, Jim Stokely, wrote for the U.S. National Park Service a book entitled, *Highland Homeland: The People of the Great Smokies*. The beautifully written and illustrated volume traces the early settlement of the Smokies, first by the powerful Cherokees and, later, by Anglo-Americans.

Along the way, the author team provides a totally readable, yet informative, look at the way things used to be in the mountains and how twentieth-century progress has had its impact on the once-blissful life of the residents of southern Appalachia.

Now, with these two titles in mind, let's think a moment about some examples for future books. The first one that comes to mind is a history of the long and varied life of the Franklin Interurban Electric Railroad which provided commuter service between Franklin and Nashville for nearly fifty years before it was replaced by buses in 1941. Another subject that is a natural for book-length treatment is a history of the iron industry in Middle Tennessee's western Highland Rim region, from its beginnings in the late 1700s till its demise well into the twentieth century. And, wouldn't the coal mine strikes in East Tennessee during the 1920s and 1930s be an interesting and meaningful subject to research and to document? Or, the National Field Trial bird dog competition that has drawn national attention to Grand Junction in Hardeman County for many, many years?

But there's more to this than just coming up with a subject. What do you want to know about it? For example, if you were to choose the Franklin Interurban Electric Railroad as your subject because of your interest in the history of transportation, you might want to know how people traveled between Franklin and Nashville before the railroad, how an electric railroad worked, what the advantages and the disadvantages were, why it was replaced by buses, and how the automobile figured in. Or if you were more interested in the role of the railroad in linking the two cities, then you would want to find out how much establishing this commuter service changed the relationship between Nashville and Franklin, whether one benefited more than the other, how it affected their growth and development. In other words, there are many different ways to approach any subject, and it is important to think on the front end about what your interest is and what questions you want to answer in your research and writing. You may change your mind later and decide you are interested in different questions, but you have to have a place to start. And the best questions are not easily answered—they ask "Why?" and "How?" and lead to more than just telling a story, describing a place, or filling in the gaps in our knowledge. But asking such questions on the front end is the key to achieving the goal of all history—local or otherwise—to help us better understand the past.

An editorial writer for *Scribner's Magazine*, whose name, unfortunately, has become lost in time, shared the excitement of researching and writing local history with his readers. In 1910, he wrote the following:

> You take a house or a bit of land, a road, or a river or Indian treaty, as a nucleus; and as you read old books, newspapers, and letters; examine old maps, plans, and pictures; and as you talk with old residents—your facts form layer after layer around your centre; and as you compare and generalize and let your imagination flow over all, your house

or bit of land, or road, or river, or Indian treaty grows and crystallizes into a shapely, lasting concretion of local history.

Wow! What more can be said to answer the question, "What shall I write about?" We think you know. Now, why not go out there and do it?

How Do You Get Organized? 3

The heroes of the Rocky Mountain fur trade were called *mountain men*, and these rugged individuals who hailed from all sections of the country and came from all walks of life were so attuned to the vast wilderness of the American West that, in many cases, they were more Indian-like in their mannerisms and survival skills than the Indians themselves. The element in most mountain men's lives that made them such survivors was the fact that they lived off the land and literally carried on their persons, or on the backs of one or two horses, everything they owned or ever hoped to possess. Much of the smaller paraphernalia—fishing line, hooks, extra flints, balls, patches, and such—they carried with them in something they called a *possible sack*, which was remarkably similar to a modern-day lady's handbag. We maintain that every good writer, just like every good mountain man of the last century, needs a possible sack in which to cart belongings when he or she goes to the library or on some other research mission.

How Do You Get Organized?

What "possibles" should be carried? Well, here's our list. Of course, over time, you'll develop your own that fits your needs. First, you have to have a well-made, roomy—but, not overly burdensome—briefcase or satchel, or whatever you want to call it. Ideally, the case should be divided into several compartments, large and small, in order to carry writing supplies and file research papers and cards. What it really boils down to is the fact that you need a kind of mini-office in which you can conveniently carry everything you need for a complete research outing. Here's a list of items that you may want to consider for your possible sack:

- ✔ A couple of yellow, 8 1/2 X 11 inch, lined tablets. Yellow is much easier on the eyes than stark white paper.

- ✔ Two or three extra pens and pencils, along with a small, hand-held pencil sharpener.

- ✔ An eraser.

- ✔ An ample supply of index cards, if you like to use them for your reference notes.

- ✔ A miniature stapler and a supply of extra staples.

- ✔ A small box containing paper clips, rubber bands, a small tube of liquid paper glue, and a pair of small scissors.

- ✔ A twelve–inch ruler.

✔ A role of transparent tape.

✔ A few sheets of graph paper.

✔ A full-sized (8 1/2 X 11 inch) page magnifier (some of the print in older material is extremely hard to read).

✔ A small tape recorder and extra tapes. If you have an involved document that is so fragile it will not copy, it's much quicker and easier to read the document into a tape recorder than it is to write every word down.

✔ Plenty of change for the copy machine. Most institutions now have bill changers, but many times during periods of high activity, they are frequently out of change. Also, some libraries provide a copy card which you can purchase for, say, five dollars. You then can use the card for five dollars worth of copying and not have all that loose change to worry about.

✔ A small dictionary and a thesaurus.

✔ Several file folders in which you can file different types of notes, etc.

✔ A supply of pressure–sensitive mailing labels. If you need to copy a number of addresses to whom you will later write for additional information, copy the addresses directly on the labels and use them on your envelopes when you mail your letters.

✔ And, finally, if you have the desire or the where-with-all, a lap-top personal computer (notebook or sub-notebook) with a good word processing package. Forget wagging around the printer. All you're after now is a speedy way of recording information.

You may also want to pack a small lunch. Our experience has been that, once you find a parking space at a research library, it's better to eat a sand-wich in the car than run the risk of losing the space.

Now, having given you all of these wonderful ideas about what to carry with you on your next research expedition, let us add one additional comment. Because of concerns about protecting research materials from possible damage, some facil-ities will not allow you to carry such items as tape, scissors, and glue or even ink pens into their refer-ence rooms. Others don't seem to mind. Most prohibit bringing any food or beverages into their facilities. To prevent embarrassment and the possi-bility of not being allowed to carry on your research, always call ahead of time and check on the policy of the facility you intend to visit.

How Do You Get Started? 4

At the risk of sounding corny—since it has been written so many times before—a writer's best friends really are the books and publications that have already been produced by numerous other authors who have followed the same lines of research. These many books were written by someone like yourself to be read and for knowledge to be gleaned from them, so take full advantage of them before you do anything else.

Do not go off half-cocked and jump right into the writing phase of a local history project—or, for that matter, any other type of project—without thoroughly investigating what has already been researched and written about the topic at hand. In many cases, particularly as it pertains to local history, you will find that the field is broad enough but the previously conducted research and documentation sparse enough, that in no way are you restricted from adding your own opus to the list of published works. However, once in a great while, you just might find that the particular subject that you had in mind to write about has been worn into the ground already, and that the addition of one more item upon its trampled grave serves no real purpose at all. And, in any case, make sure to check out footnotes and bibliographies—they often provide invaluable leads to other publications and sources that you will want to use in your own project.

One of the best and quickest ways to determine what is already out there would be to refer to some monster, up-to-date, all-comprehensive bibliography that covered all aspects of Tennessee history. Unfortunately, such a volume does not exist. However, information contained in various other books and kept fairly well up-to-date in the larger libraries across the state can go a long way in helping you gauge, not only what is available for assisting you in your own research, but the potential success, based upon other works already published, you might expect for your publication project at hand.

Let's look at a few of these works, keeping in mind that the chances your local library might have them are remote. And, since they are mostly reference books, its doubtful you'll be able to get them on inter-library loan. The Tennessee State Library and Archives in Nashville maintains copies of most, however, and the larger city institutions across the state, as well as the Mormon facilities, probably house copies as well. (*See* chapter 5.)

One last point to remember. Because massive volumes like the works we are considering here usually turn out to be years-long projects, are extremely expensive to update and republish even every few years, and are usually laboriously updated and edited by someone more for love than for money, they might appear to be out-of-date before they ever leave the press. In many cases, this is a correct assumption. But, don't be discouraged by the publication date on some of these books. If you find some of the titles in major libraries across the state, the chances are they are the latest editions available regardless of the two- or-three-years-ago-or-more-date on the title page. Use them; they are the nearest thing to comprehensiveness we, as writers of local history, have.

The first book to which an aspiring writer of Tennessee local history should refer is Sam B. Smith's *Tennessee History: A Bibliography*, published in 1974 by the University of Tennessee at Knoxville. Yes, it is dated, but it is being updated and prepared for reissue. Perhaps by the time you read these words, this valuable volume will again be available.

The beauty in Smith's book lies in the manner in which it is organized. After an excellent narrative about the historical literature of the state in general, the volume is divided into major headings and subheadings, such as "Andrew Jackson," or "Reconstruction," or "Natural History," or one of many more categories. Completing the nearly five-hundred-page reference is an individual county-by-county listing of books, magazine articles, and unpublished manuscripts regarding each governmental entity. Plus, the book is capped off with both author and subject indices and a listing of the ninety-five county historians.

Next in value to writers of Tennessee history are the published indices of the *Tennessee Historical Quarterly* and its predecessors, the *Tennessee Historical Magazine* and the *American Historical Magazine*. The nearly four hundred different issues of these three journals, published under the auspices of

16

the Tennessee Historical Society over the past one hundred years, contain a virtual treasure house of information and articles relative to all aspects of Tennessee local and regional history. Obviously, the present-day researcher and writer should likewise utilize the indices to similar publications issued by the East Tennessee Historical Society and the West Tennessee Historical Society.

Listed below are more reference volumes we believe will be of tremendous value to anyone researching Tennessee history. The books are listed here in no particular order of potential importance, but rather alphabetically by the author's, editor's, or compiler's last name.

Abate, Frank R., ed. *Omni Gazetteer of the United States of America.* Detroit: Omnigraphics, Inc., 1991. Sooner or later in your research, you will most likely be required to refer to maps and gazetteers of Tennessee in order to locate natural features, obscure rivers and streams, and other geographical data. This gazetteer is the granddaddy of them all. A massive eleven-volume set, volume 4, pages 831-1156 contains the Tennessee material that could be invaluable to you during your research phase. Case in point: Suppose you run across an item that refers to Spring Branch. All you know is that taken in context with your historical research, Spring Branch is a small creek, but you're not sure where. This gazetteer shows you that there are eighteen "Spring Branches" located in Tennessee ranging from Bradley County in the east to Benton County in the west, and it gives you the latitude/longitude coordinates and the U.S. Geological Survey topographical map sector in which each one is located.

CIS U.S. Serial Set Index. Washington, D.C.: Congressional Information Service, Inc., 1975–. This multi-volume set instructs you on how to easily access literally thousands upon thousands of official U.S. documents that have been published over the years, including the very valuable (for local researchers and writers) *American State Papers* documented from the 15th–34th Congresses, 1789–1857, including U.S. Senate Executive Documents and Reports, and Presidential Executive Orders and Proclamations.

Corbitt, David Leroy. *The Formation of the North Carolina Counties 1663–1943.* Raleigh: State Department of Archives and History, 1950. This engaging book gives the historical background of the establishment of North Carolina counties, including those now in Tennessee but which at the time of their formation were part of North Carolina, i.e., Davidson, Greene, Hawkins, Sullivan, Sumner, and Washington.

Corlew, Robert E. *Tennessee: A Short History.* 2d ed. Knoxville: University of Tennessee Press, 1981. First published in 1969, this one-volume history provides the best overview of the state's history with suggested readings for each chapter.

Crane, Sophie and Paul, *Tennessee Taproots: Courthouses of Tennessee,* Bicentennial Edition, Franklin: Providence House Publishers, 1996. First published in 1976, this updated bicentennial edition includes new color photographs and a listing of Tennessee's state and county historians.

18

Cross, Wallace, comp. *Bibliography on Local History for the Following 13 Middle Tennessee Counties: Benton, Cheatham, Dickson, Hickman, Houston, Humphreys, Montgomery, Perry, Robertson, Stewart, Sumner, Trousdale, Williamson.* A Tennessee Community Heritage Project, 1984. This brief booklet simply lists publishing information about books and pamphlets of historical interest as they pertain to the listed counties.

Dissertation Abstracts. Ann Arbor, Michigan: University Microfilms International, 1993. UMI's database of one million dissertations is available on three CD–ROMs, covering dissertations produced between 1861 and 1992. This database can be searched electronically by any word or group of words and thus provides better access than paper versions with more traditional indexing.

Filby, P. William, comp. *A Bibliography of American County Histories.* Baltimore: Genealogical Publishing Company, Inc., 1985. This book, updated through December 1984, contains information regarding five thousand published American county histories.

Gibson, Arrell Morgan. *The American Indian: Prehistory to the Present.* Lexington, Mass.: D.C. Heath, 1980. A basic introduction to the Native American experience.

Grundset, Eric G. and Antolin, Ana. *Library Catalog.* Vol. 2, *State and Local Histories and Records.* Washington, D.C.: National Society of the Daughters of the American Revolution, 1986. This reference describes the DAR's Washington, D.C., library collection, containing more than twenty-three thousand books on general and local history. The Tennessee material is listed on pages 564 to 583.

Heitman, Francis B. *Historical Register and Dictionary of the United States Army, from Its Organization, September 29, 1789, to March 2, 1903.* 2 vols. Washington, D.C.: Government Printing Office, 1903. In addition to containing the name and unit data on every officer who served in the U.S. Army to the turn of the century, the book contains a vast amount of information on early forts, the organizational makeup of the Army, and other important listings.

Kaminkow, Marion J., ed. *United States Local Histories in the Library of Congress: A Bibliography.* Baltimore: Magna Carta Book Company, 1975. The Tennessee entries in this massive, five-volume set of books are found in volume 3 (main entries) and volume 5 (supplementary entries).

Kane, Joseph Nathan. *The American Counties.* 4th ed. Metuchen, New Jersey: Scarecrow Press, 1983. This volume presents listings and information about all U.S. counties in the following formats: by county, by state, by date of establishment, for whom or what named, county seats, independent cities, and a list of counties whose names have changed.

Kuehl, Warren F. *Dissertations in History: An Index to Dissertations Completed in History Departments of United States and Canadian Institutions.* Vol. 1, *1873–1960.* Lexington: University of Kentucky Press,

179   Reid, John.
　　　　　Connecticut, from the best authorities.　₍New York, 1796₎
　　　　　"B. Tanner del. & sculpt.　Engraved for the American Edition
　　　　　of Winterbotham's History of America, Published by John Reid."
　　　　　₍From American atlas, New York, published by John Reid, 1796,
　　　　　known as atlas to Winterbotham's history₎.
　　　　　　　Scale ca. 1:400,000.　15 x 17-1/2 in.
　　　　　　　County and township boundaries are indicated.
　　　　　　　A line symbol with name alongside indicates this route:
　　　　　　　　Post road ₍Boston post road₎ (from Greenwich through
　　　　　　　　　New Haven and New London towards Boston)
　　　　　　　Other routes are shown by line symbol without name.

180   Rhea, Matthew.
　　　　　Map of the state of Tennessee, taken from survey by Matthew
　　　　　Rhea.　Published by the author, Columbia, Tenn.　Engraved by
　　　　　H.S. Tanner, E.B. Dawson & J. Knight, Philadelphia.　Sold by
　　　　　H.S. Tanner, Philadelphia, Eichbaum & Norvell, Nashville, &
　　　　　S.D. Jacobs, Knoxville.　c1832.
　　　　　　　Scale ca. 1:450,000.　In 3 parts: 2 parts, each 35 x 17
　　　　　in.; 1 part, 35 x 35 in.　In colors.
　　　　　　　Distinguishing line symbols are shown for "Important Roads"
　　　　　and "Common Roads."　The legend also includes state and county
　　　　　lines, Indian boundary lines, old forts and Indian villages.

181   Road Builders' News.
　　　　　National Pike or Cumberland Road.　₍1938₎　In Road Builders'
　　　　　News ₍Apr., 1938₎ page 8 (at bottom).　This map and 12 views
　　　　　(reproductions from photographs and old prints) illustrate
　　　　　article by Albert C. Rose, "The National Pike or Cumberland
　　　　　Road" (pages 8-14, each 11 x 8-1/2 in.).
　　　　　　　Scale ca. 1:10,000,000.　2 x 6-1/2 in.
　　　　　　　A legend on the map contains distinctive line symbols for
　　　　　portions of the pike "completed by the United States" (from
　　　　　Cumberland, Md., to Springfield, Ohio), "partly completed"
　　　　　(from Springfield, Ohio, to Vandalia, Ill.), and "projected"
　　　　　(from Vandalia, Ill., to Jefferson City, Mo.), 1806-1824.

182   Robinson, Lewis.
　　　　　An improved map of Vermont.　Compiled from the latest authorities.
　　　　　Reading, 1840.
　　　　　　　Scale ca. 1:450,000.　24-1/2 x 17-1/2 in.
　　　　　　　County boundaries are shown by colors.
　　　　　　　To the left of the map (but within the dimensions given
　　　　　above) is a tabulation of names of towns, within counties,

73

Figure 1. Reference page from Maps Showing Explorer's Routes, Trails, and Early Roads in the United States, *compiled by Richard S. Ladd, Washington, D.C.: Library of Congress, 1962.*

1965. Vol. 2, *1961-1970*. Lexington: University Press of Kentucky, 1972. Vol. 3, *1970-1980*. Santa Barbara, California: Clio Information Services, 1985. This informative set contains the titles, authorship information, locations, and synopses of thousands of unpublished university dissertations, many of them dealing with specific issues of local and state history, including Tennessee-oriented subjects.

Ladd, Richard S., comp. *Maps Showing Explorers' Routes, Trails, and Early Roads in the United States*. Washington, D.C.: Library of Congress, 1962. The title says it all. This book is obviously invaluable to those needing assistance in locating ancient landmarks, extinct villages and towns, and early highway data for selected regions. See Figure 1 for an illustration of a representative page that refers to a Tennessee map.

Milhollen, Hirst D. and Mugridge, Donald H., comps. *Civil War Photographs, 1861-1865*. Washington, D.C.: Reference Department, Library of Congress, 1961. This book is a catalog of the historic photographs made during the Civil War by the famed photographer Mathew B. Brady and his disciples that are now housed at the Library of Congress. Tennessee material includes photos from the Chattanooga campaign, the siege of Knoxville, Hood's Nashville campaign, and many generic war shots and portraits of both United States' and Confederate States' leaders and military commanders.

Moore, Mrs. John Trotwood. *Record of Commissions of Officers in the Tennessee Militia, 1796-1815*. Baltimore:

MS 85-820

Loyal Tennesseans League.
Records, 1932. – 1 carton.
In: Memphis State University Library, Mississippi Valley Collection (Tenn.).
Formed to support re-election of Governor Malcolm R. Patterson of Tennessee in the Democratic primary of Aug. 3, 1932. – Correspondence and individual and group applications for membership.
Anonymous gift.
Finding aid published in: National Inventory of Documentary Sources in the United States, microfiche 4.91.61.

MS 85-821

Meeman, Edward J. (Edward John), 1889-1966.
Papers, 1931-1966. – 25 cu. ft.
In: Memphis State University Library, Mississippi Valley Collection (Tenn.) (Mss 85).
Editor of the Press-Scimitar, Memphis, Tenn.
Professional research files (correspondence, clippings, and notes) concerning conservation of natural resources, politics at the national and local levels, and other topics. Includes material on Tennessee Valley Authority; the political organization of Edward Hull Crump and its eventual defeat by Estes Kefauver, whom Meeman supported; Great Smoky Mountains National Park; election reform; and human relations.
Gifts of Edward Orgill, 1973, and Edwin Howard, 1980.
Finding aid published in: National Inventory of Documentary Sources in the United States, microfiche 4.91.63.

MS 85-822

Memphis Power and Light Company (Tenn.)
Records, 1898-1950. – 20 cu. ft.
In: Memphis State University Library, Mississippi Valley Collection (Tenn.).
Formed 1922; disbanded 1939, when Memphis Light, Gas, and Water Division was formed.
Correspondence (1898-1950) and general office and business files (1897-1950) of the company and related organizations, including Memphis Gas and Electric Company, that have provided electric power to Memphis; together with documents of Fourth Street Electric Steam Station (1927-1941). Other organizations represented include Arkansas Power and Light Company, Memphis Generating Company, Tennessee Valley Authority, Federal Power Commission, Memphis Natural Gas Company, and Railroad and Public Utilities Commission of Tennessee.
Gift of Tennessee Valley Authority Archives, Chattanooga, Tenn., via Ronald Brewer, 1983.
Finding aid published in: National Inventory of Documentary Sources in the United States, microfiche 4.91.67.

MS 85-823

National Organization for Women. Memphis Chapter (Tenn.)
Records, 1971-1983. – 5 cu. ft.
In: Memphis State University Library, Mississippi Valley Collection (Tenn.).
Chartered 1971. – Administrative and membership records and publications; chapter files, including clippings, correspondence, financial and other records, and legal documents; and oral history interview (1982) of former chapter president Phyllis Dougherty.
Gift of the chapter. Additions expected.
Finding aid published in: National Inventory of Documentary Sources in the United States, microfiche 4.91.70

MS 85-824

Odle, H. D.
Business ledger, 1903-1909. – 1 v.
In: Memphis State University Library, Mississippi Valley Collection (Tenn.).
Businessman. – Record of purchases and disbursements of a rural general store operated by Odle.
Purchased from Mattie Burkholder, 1971.
Finding aid published in: National Inventory of Documentary Sources in the United States, microfiche 4.91.71.

MS 85-825

Reynolds, Dyer Marion, 1930-1980.
Circus collection, 1878-1980. – 75 cartons.
In: Memphis State University Library, Mississippi Valley Collection (Tenn.).
Collector, nicknamed "Ichabod" by his circus associates, who worked with Ringling Brothers (1951-1956) and devoted the remainder of his life to collecting and preserving circus material.
Business and personal correspondence of Reynolds, and clippings, handbills, publications, scrapbooks, and memorabilia, documenting all aspects of the history and operation of circuses, including Ringling Brothers Barnum and Bailey, Al G. Barnes Circus, and many others; together with papers of Reynolds's friend and associate Edward Riggs ("Whitey") Veersteeg (1900-1969), electrician in the entertainment business and head of Ringling Brothers' electrical department.
Gift of Mr. Reynolds, Los Angeles, Calif., 1969 and 1980.
Finding aid published in: National Inventory of Documentary Sources in the United States, microfiche 4.91.14.

MS 85-826

Southern Tenant Farmers' Union.
Ephemera, 1934-1963. – 1 carton.
In: Memphis State University Library, Mississippi Valley Collection (Tenn.).
Organized 1934; reorganized 1946 as National Farm Labor Union; in 1952 became National Agricultural Workers Union, which in 1960 joined Amalgamated Meat Cutters and Butcher Workers of North America. – Reports, articles, speeches, and clippings, relating to significant events in the history of the union, including legal brief of the 1935 test case against Arkansas plantation owner Hiram Norcross; together with transcripts of oral history interviews conducted by H.L. Mitchell, a founder and president, and articles by Mitchell and others.
Gift of A. Eugene Cox, Memphis, Tenn., 1968.
Finding aid published in: National Inventory of Documentary Sources in the United States, microfiche 4.91.86.

MS 85-827

Stahl, E. M.
Civil War diaries, 1863-1865. – 3 v.
In: Memphis State University Library, Mississippi Valley Collection (Tenn.).
Soldier, of Hartford, Ill. – Diaries describing the experiences of Stahl, of 84th Illinois Volunteer Infantry Regiment, while stationed in and around Franklin, Tenn.
Purchased from Mattie Burkholder, 1971.
Finding aid in the repository. .

Figure 2. Reference page from National Union Catalog of Manuscript Collections, *Washington, D.C.: Library of Congress, 1992.*

Genealogical Publishing Company, 1977. If your writing carries you into the military annals of early statehood, a good reference is the above title by an eminent authority on Tennessee history.

Morris, Eastin. *The Tennessee Gazetteer, or Topographical Dictionary.* Nashville: W. Hasell Hunt & Co., 1834. Reprinted as McBride, Robert M. and Meredith, Owen, editors. Nashville: The Gazetteer Press, 1971. This tiny book is an absolute gem. Tennessee is frozen in time in the early 1830s as you read the delightful descriptions of towns, rivers, steamship and stagecoach routes, and listings of state and national office-holders. Of immense importance to historical researchers.

National Union Catalog of Manuscript Collections. Washington, D.C.: Library of Congress, 1959–93. This valuable multi-volume publication describes more than seven hundred thousand manuscript collections, housed in depositories across the United States. See Figure 2 for an illustration of a representative entry about a Tennessee item.

Records of Officers and Men of the Tennessee National Guard, 1921–1941. Nashville, 1944. This multi-volume compendium gives critical information on every member of the Tennessee National Guard who served between the years 1921–1941. Data included are: name, date of birth, place of birth, date of enlistment, place of enlistment, grade (rank), company and regiment, discharge date, character, remarks, and special orders.

in the Library of Congress (Washington, Library of Congress, 1973), v. 7, no. 10671.

396.2

Von Reizenstein, B., *and* F. D'Avignon.

Western Tennessee, and part of Kentucky. Prepared by order of Capt. McAlester, Chief Engr. M.D.W.M. under direction of Capt. P. C. Hains, U. S. Engr. & Actg. Chief Engr. Dept. of the Gulf. Compiled & drawn for stone by B. von Reizenstein, & F. D'Avignon. Printed by E. Boehler. Feb. 1865. Uncolored. Scale 1:633,600. 41 × 65 cm.

At head of title: Engineer's Office, Department of the Gulf. Map no. 55.

"Authorities: U. S. Coast Surveys, & Lloyd's military map."

Indicates cities and towns, forts, roads, railroads, rivers, and some relief by hachures.

396.25

Weyss, John E., John Earhart, *and* William H. Greenwood.

Topographical sketch of the country adjacent to the turnpike between Nolensville and Chapel Hill, Tenn. Compiled from original reconnoissances [sic] under the direction of Capt. N. Michler, Topographical Engrs. U.S.A. By Major J. E. Weyss, Capt. John Earhart, Lieut. W. Greenwood. [1863?] Photocopy (positive). Scale ca. 1:72,500 (not "1 mile to the inch"). 59 × 33 cm.

Hand-colored photocopy of parts of Williamson, Marshall, Rutherford, and Bedford counties, Tennessee, indicating roads, towns, distances, rivers, houses and names of residents, and relief by hachures.

BLUE SPRINGS

396.3

Blue Springs [Tennessee. October 10, 1863] Colored ms. Scale ca. 1:15,840 ("about 4 in. to 1 mile"). 48 × 29 cm.

G3964.B57S5 1863.B4 Vault

Rough pencil sketch showing the position of "Willcox Reserve" (i.e., Gen. Orlando B. Willcox). Map has been partially traced in ink on the verso.

From the papers of Gen. Orlando M. Poe, Manuscript Division, L.C.

CAMP BRENTWOOD

396.35

Smith, Anson S.

[Sketch map of Camp Brentwood, Tennessee, while serving as quarters for the 86th and 104th regiments of the Illinois volunteers] Ans. Smith, Brentwood, Tenn., June: 1863. Colored ms. Scale not given. 25 × 40 cm.

G3964.B76:2C3S5 1863 .S4 Vault

This pen and ink sketch map, drawn by Anson S. Smith, Co. D, 104th regiment, Illinois volunteers, shows earthworks, ditches, abatis, gun emplacements, rifle pits, campgrounds, the Louisville and Nashville Railroad, and the nearby Harpeth River. Smith describes the colors used and how to interpret the map as follows: "Red for all dirt thrown up for redoubts & breast work, black for ditches & rifle pits, 2 rows of brush & limbs from trees for the abattus [sic] of which there are 2 rows around or nearly around the fort. Guess at what you dont know as that is the way that I do." The map is drawn on the verso of a letter from Smith dated June 3, 1863, to John J. Taylor, La Salle Co., Illinois. Smith notes in his letter that "I have just come in from picket & the fort that I have started to draw for you is all torn to hell, the banks & breast works are all all [sic] leveled to the ground. Convalescents are ordered to report to the Doctor at 2 oclock. I suppose we will march for Franklin or Collumbia [sic] or some place toward the front tonight & skedaddle from here."

CANEY FORK

396.4

Weyss, John E.

Sketch of the vicinity of the falls of Caney Fork of Cumberland River, Ten. Constructed from information received of W. Bosson Esq. under the direction of Capt. N. Michler, Topl. Engrs. U.S.A., by John E. Weyss, Maj. Ky. Vols. April 1863. Photocopy (positive). Scale ca. 1:31,680. 9 × 22 cm.

Hand-colored photocopy of parts of Warren and Van Buren counties, Tennessee, indicating rivers, falls, roads, houses and names of residents, woodland, and relief by hachures.

CHATTANOOGA

396.6

American Heritage Publishing Company.

The American Heritage battle map of Chattanooga. [Drawn by] David Greenspan. [New York] ©1961. Colored view. Not drawn to scale. 39 × 59 cm.

Bird's-eye view showing principal sites and events of the battles of Orchard Knob, Lookout Mountain, and Missionary Ridge.

397

Badeau, Adam.

Battle of Chattanooga, Nov. 23, 24, 25, 1863. Uncol-

Figure 3. Reference page from Civil War Maps: An Annotated List of Maps and Atlases in the Library of Congress, *Second Edition, compiled by Richard W. Stephenson, Washington, D.C.: Library of Congress, 1989.*

Stephenson, Richard W., comp. *Civil War Maps: An Annotated List of Maps and Atlases in the Library of Congress.* Washington, D.C.: Library of Congress, 1989. If your field of research and writing is the Civil War era, this book can be of tremendous assistance not only in helping you locate places now long gone, but as an illustration resource as well. Refer to Figure 3 for a Tennessee-related page from this well-organized and valuable reference.

Sturtevant, William C., gen. ed. *The Handbook of North American Indians.* Washington, D.C.: Smithsonian Institution Press, 1978–1990. This multi–volume publication is one of the most useful resources on North American Indian life, the various tribes, their original locations, mores, lifestyles, etc.

Tennessee Blue Book 1995–1996, Bicentennial Edition (1796–1996), Nashville: State of Tennessee, 1996. This volume contains an expanded and completely revised history section and a special focus on the state's bicentennial celebration

White, Virgil D. *Index to Volunteer Soldiers in Indian Wars and Disturbances, 1815–1858.* 2 vols. Waynesboro, Tennessee: National Historical Publishing Company, 1994. This volume contains the names and other information of every soldier who ever volunteered his services during any of the U.S. government's conflicts with the Indians. White has also published indices to Revolutionary War service records, War of 1812 pension files, Mexican War pension files, and other records that you may want to investigate.

Where Can You Go for Help? 5

Avariety of institutions offer assistance and maintain collections that will prove critical to your local history research. You will probably need to visit several of these facilities as you conduct your research, but in some cases you may be able to find out what you need to know by telephone or letter. The following are the ones we believe will be of most use to you.

LIBRARIES AND ARCHIVAL HOLDINGS

NATIONAL ARCHIVES AND RECORDS ADMINISTRATION (NARA)
Seventh Street and Pennsylvania Avenue, NW
Washington, D.C. 20408
(202) 501-5400, and,
8601 Adelphi Road
College Park, Maryland 20740–6001
(301) 713–6800

The National Archives and Records Administration (NARA) establishes policies and procedures for managing all U.S. government records. It also accessions, preserves, and makes available to the public a variety of historically valuable records of the government. NARA maintains a massive and complex collection of historical data from many regions, eras, and areas of our national experience, spanning the time period from the Revolutionary War to the present. Its holdings in military history are especially noteworthy. The Military Section houses individual records of men and women who have served in the U.S. Army, Navy, Marine Corps, Coast Guard, Air Force, and Confederate States armed forces, as well as volunteer military service in the federal interest.

In addition to the main archives in Washington, D.C., and College Park, Maryland, NARA maintains several regional research centers, which house the papers and records of field offices of federal agencies, including U.S. courts, that are or were located in the states served by that region. The regional research center that serves Tennessee is:

National Archives and Records Administration—
Southeast Region (NARA-SE)
1557 St. Joseph Avenue
East Point, Georgia 30344
(404) 763-7477

To attempt to explain—even if we could, which we can't— which office has which records would require many times the space that we have in this book to give. We advise that you call or write the Washington, D.C., or College Park, Maryland, offices for military-related matters or the Atlanta office for court and other federal agency-related matters. Information on the Archives' collections is also available online through the NARA World–Wide Web page.

ORDER FOR COPIES OF VETERANS RECORDS
(See Instructions page before completing this form)

DATE RECEIVED IN NNRG

INDICATE BELOW THE TYPE OF FILE DESIRED AND THE METHOD OF PAYMENT PREFERRED.

1. FILE TO BE SEARCHED
(Check one box only)
- ☐ PENSION
- ☐ BOUNTY-LAND WARRANT APPLICATION *(Service before 1856 only)*
- ☐ MILITARY

2. PAYMENT METHOD *(Check one box only)*

☐ CREDIT CARD *(VISA or MasterCard)* for IMMEDIATE SHIPMENT of copies

Account Number.
Exp. Date:

Signature:
Daytime Phone:

☐ BILL ME *(No Credit Card)*

REQUIRED MINIMUM IDENTIFICATION OF VETERAN - MUST BE COMPLETED OR YOUR ORDER CANNOT BE SERVICED

3. VETERAN *(Give last, first, and middle names)*

4. BRANCH OF SERVICE IN WHICH HE SERVED
☐ ARMY   ☐ NAVY   ☐ MARINE CORPS

5. STATE FROM WHICH HE SERVED

6. WAR IN WHICH, OR DATES BETWEEN WHICH, HE SERVED

7. IF SERVICE WAS CIVIL WAR
☐ UNION   ☐ CONFEDERATE

PLEASE PROVIDE THE FOLLOWING ADDITIONAL INFORMATION, IF KNOWN

8. UNIT IN WHICH HE SERVED *(Name of regiment or number, company, etc, name of ship)*

9. IF SERVICE WAS ARMY, ARM IN WHICH HE SERVED
☐ INFANTRY   ☐ CAVALRY   ☐ ARTILLERY
If other, specify:

Rank
☐ OFFICER   ☐ ENLISTED

10. KIND OF SERVICE
☐ VOLUNTEERS   ☐ REGULARS

11. PENSION/BOUNTY-LAND FILE NO.

12. IF VETERAN LIVED IN A HOME FOR SOLDIERS, GIVE LOCATION *(City and State)*

13. PLACE(S) VETERAN LIVED AFTER SERVICE

14. DATE OF BIRTH

15. PLACE OF BIRTH *(City, County, State, etc.)*

16. NAME OF WIDOW OR OTHER CLAIMANT

16. DATE OF DEATH

17. PLACE OF DEATH *(City, County, State, etc.)*

NATIONAL ARCHIVES TRUST FUND BOARD   NATF Form 80 (rev. 4-92)

DO NOT WRITE BELOW - SPACE IS FOR OUR REPLY TO YOU

☐ **NO--We were unable to locate the file you requested above. No payment is required.**

DATE SEARCHED   SEARCHER

☐ **REQUIRED MINIMUM IDENTIFICATION OF VETERAN WAS NOT PROVIDED.** Please complete blocks 3 (give full name), 4, 5, 6, and 7 and resubmit your order.

☐ **A SEARCH WAS MADE BUT THE FILE YOU REQUESTED ABOVE WAS NOT FOUND.** When we do not find a record for a veteran, this does not mean that he did not serve. You may be able to obtain information about him from the archives of the State from which he served.

☐ See attached forms, leaflets, or information sheets.

☐ **YES--We located the file you requested above. We have made copies from the file for you. The cost for these copies is $10.**

DATE SEARCHED   SEARCHER

FILE DESIGNATION

Make your check or money order payable to NATIONAL ARCHIVES TRUST FUND. Do not send cash. Return this form and your payment in the enclosed envelope to:

NATIONAL ARCHIVES TRUST FUND
P.O. BOX 100221
ATLANTA, GA 30384-0221

PLEASE NOTE: We will hold these copies awaiting receipt of payment for only 45 days from the date completed, which is stamped below. After that time, you must submit another form to obtain photocopies of the file.

THIS IS YOUR MAILING LABEL. PRESS FIRMLY.

NAME *(Last, First, MI)*

STREET

CITY, STATE

ZIP CODE

(A677973)

INVOICE/REPLY COPY - DO NOT DETACH

National Archives and Records Administration (NARA) form for ordering copies of veterans' records.

LIBRARY OF CONGRESS (LC)
First Street and Independence Avenue, SE
Washington, D.C. 20540
(202) 707-5000

The Library of Congress (LC) had its beginnings nearly two hundred years ago when Thomas Jefferson sold his personal library at Monticello to the U.S. government to be used as the core for a national library. Since then, the institution has grown to house one of the world's truly magnificent collections of books, manuscripts, photographs, maps, and other archival material.

As the overseer of the U.S. Copyright Office, the LC gets a shot at every book published in the United States, a vast number of which it incorporates into its collections. Its historical holdings are far too extensive to discuss here; however, a good overview guide to the institution and what it contains can be found in *The Library of Congress: A Guide to Genealogical and Historical Research* by James C. Neagles, published in 1990 by Ancestry Publishing Company of Salt Lake City, Utah. The LC also runs a World–Wide Web page with information about the library and access to its card catalog. The Library of Congress maintains a huge local history collection, so don't hesitate to contact its personnel as you research your own book.

Where Can You Go for Help?

NATIONAL SOCIETY OF THE DAUGHTERS OF THE AMERICAN REVOLUTION (DAR) LIBRARY
Constitution Hall
1776 D Street, NW
Washington, D.C. 20006
(202) 628–1776

The Daughters of the American Revolution (DAR) records make a valuable contribution to historical research. The DAR Library is open to the public, but charges a fee to non-DAR members. It contains more than twenty-three thousand general and local history volumes.

THE CHURCH OF JESUS CHRIST OF LATTER-DAY SAINTS (LDS)
Family History Support Office
Joseph Smith Building
15 East South Temple
Salt Lake City, Utah 84150
(800) 324-6044

One of the best-kept secrets among family and local historians is the fact that the Mormon Church maintains family history centers in Tennessee. For years, this church has been recognized for the maintenance of the largest collection of local material in the nation (the equivalent of five million volumes in hard copy or on microfilm) at its LDS Family History Library in Salt Lake City, Utah. Now, with the establishment of local centers, access for the public is much more convenient, with some providing access via computer and/or microfilm to practically all of the records that are maintained in Salt Lake City. This includes a wide variety of genealogical materials, as well as local

THE TENNESSEE GRASSROOTS WRITER

history records, veterans' and court records, church histories, cemetery and census records, and much more. A detailed overview of source material located at the Family History Library can be found in *The Library: A Guide to the LDS Family History Library*, edited by Johni Cerny and Wendy Elliott, and published in 1988 by Ancestry Publishing Company of Salt Lake City.

In Tennessee, LDS family history centers are located in Chattanooga, Clarksville, Columbia, Cookeville, Franklin, Gallatin, Kingsport, Knoxville, McMinnville, Memphis, Murfreesboro, Nashville, Paris, and Tullahoma. The hours of operation of these branch libraries vary, so you would be advised to call ahead before making a visit. Further information is available from the LDS Family History Support Office in Salt Lake City.

TENNESSEE STATE LIBRARY AND ARCHIVES (TSL&A)
403 Seventh Avenue, North
Nashville, Tennessee 37243
(615) 741-2764

The Tennessee State Library and Archives (TSL&A) maintains a large and valuable collection of materials useful to the researcher of local history. Tennessee county and family histories are cataloged and are available in the main reading room. Biographical information regarding Tennesseans is found through special indeces. Manuscript material and newspaper clippings regarding local people and events are arranged for easy access. Although there is no index for Tennessee newspapers,

32

the marriage and death notices which appeared in some early newspapers have been listed and published in book form. Additionally, the TSL&A maintains a large number of Tennessee-published newspapers on microfilm.

Periodicals published by family associations, genealogical, and historical organizations are present in the library, as are guides to their content. In addition to Tennessee materials, there is a large quantity of information about the North Carolina region from which Tennessee was formed.

Individual county records (marriages, court proceedings, wills, and deeds) are on microfilm, as well as hard copy. Cemetery records, tax roles, land records, and pension data for individual counties are available. Military records include information dating from the Revolution through World War I, including Confederate service and the muster roles for soldiers who served during the Cherokee Removal.

The TSL&A maintains a large photographic collection of Tennessee-related sites and people. In the authors' opinion, if you could visit only one institution to pursue your research into local history, it would be this excellent archival repository.

CITY AND COUNTY LIBRARIES

Practically every one of Tennessee's ninety-five counties maintains its own county library. The major population centers have large and well-stocked libraries, the sum of their inventory numbering well over five million books. And most of these larger, better-endowed libraries have nice and relatively complete local history sections, such as the Nashville Room at the Nashville-Metropolitan Public Library. Obviously, however, some of the smaller county libraries are more complete and sophisticated than others, and the size and completeness of each is usually dependent upon the economic health of each county.

All counties have access to the Tennessee Regional Library System (TRLS), administered by the Tennessee State Library and Archives. The TRLS assists local public libraries in providing free library service to Tennessee citizens. There are four single-county regions consisting of Davidson, Hamilton, Knox, and Shelby counties. The remainder of the state is divided into twelve regions, each consisting of from six to nine counties with a regional library center. The regional centers, which are funded through the TSL&A, provide local libraries with books and technical assistance, while also administering bookmobile service. The regions themselves do not circulate materials; they simply put their books on indefinite loan in the local public libraries, circulating

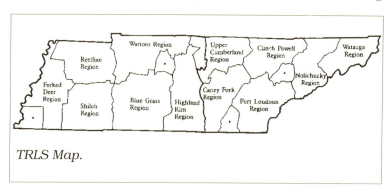

TRLS Map.

them along with the locally owned books. The accompanying map depicts the various regions contained in the TRLS network.

If your proposed book is highly localized and pertains to a community, or church, or business, or whatever in a particular county, then obviously a visit to that county's library would be the first order of the day. In many cases, you'll find a wealth of information there that can't be found anywhere else, because limited means of production and distribution have precluded authors from widely circulating their contributions. On the other hand, a small county library, because of its own limited funding, may be extremely short on the broader, historically oriented sources that you need. If that is the case, don't forget the important service provided by most libraries called "interlibrary loan."

Nowadays, you literally have the country's library system at your fingertips, with interlibrary loan services. You simply obtain the title and author of the book you desire to acquire and your local library puts out a search for it. When another library finds the book in its collection, its staff notifies your library that it has it and sends it along. You have a finite time period (a week or maybe two) to keep the book. And, the good news is the service is usually (although not always) free to you, the patron.

Here's another helpful hint: Suppose you're researching material for a biography about a particular mountain man who was born locally in 1806. You live in Wazoo County, which is small and whose library has a limited collection, and, unfortunately, no books on the "mountain man" era of American history. Find a copy of the multi-series books entitled *Books in Print*. If the library doesn't own a set, a nearby bookstore will. Look in the subject volume under the heading, "Fur Trade." Make a list of the titles that look most interesting to you and that might have value to you for background information about the life and times of generic mountain men. Then, simply go to your library and order the book or books (sometimes there is a limit to the number you can order at one time) through interlibrary loan.

COLLEGE AND UNIVERSITY LIBRARIES

There is hardly a place in Tennessee that is very far away from a college or university. Virtually each of these institutions, whether they be community colleges, religious schools, privately operated, or state-run organizations, has a library of some kind. Indeed, some of them have extensive local history holdings, such as Austin Peay State University's "Tennesseana" book collection or the Mississippi Valley Collection at the University of Memphis. For assistance in determining which college or university library might help you in your research, refer to *Library Resources in Tennessee: A Directory of Unique and Special Collections*, a 1985 publication of the Tennessee Secretary of State. These libraries are not traditionally open to the public, however, and some charge fees for access. Also, while college or university libraries may allow you to use their collections, they are unlikely under any circumstance to allow you to check out books. Obviously, you should inquire about restrictions before you visit.

HISTORICAL SOCIETIES

TENNESSEE HISTORICAL SOCIETY
War Memorial Building
Nashville, Tennessee 37219
(615) 741-8934

> The Tennessee Historical Society was chartered in 1849 as a private agency. Its membership consists of about twenty-five hundred. The society has a vast collection, but unfortunately, no place to keep it. Its artifacts, therefore, are shared with the Tennessee State Museum and its documentary collection—consisting of letters, diaries, journals, maps, family papers, manuscript materials, photographs, and books—are housed at the Tennessee State Library and Archives. What this means to you from a historical research standpoint is that when you search TSL&A, you more or less automatically search the Tennessee Historical Society's documents as well.

WEST TENNESSEE HISTORICAL SOCIETY
P. O. Box 111046
Memphis, Tennessee 38111
(901) 567-4518

> The West Tennessee Historical Society was organized in 1857 and concentrates on West Tennessee history. Its extensive Mississippi Valley Collection of papers and books is housed at the University of Memphis.

EAST TENNESSEE HISTORICAL SOCIETY
500 West Church
Knoxville, Tennessee 37902
(615) 544-5732

> Organized in 1925, the East Tennessee Historical Society currently serves some two thousand members. It publishes a historical quarterly and promotes public awareness through a variety of outreach programs, lectures, exhibits, and conferences. The Society's docu ment collection is housed with the McClung Historical Collection of the Knox County Public Library System.

In addition to having libraries, most Tennessee counties have local historical societies and county historians. However, in most cases, the collections of these variously sized organizations are housed in the county libraries, and there is no separate place to research. As a rule of thumb, whenever you visit a specific county library, your first question should be whether or not the county supports a historical society, and if so, where the document collection resides.

CHURCH HISTORICAL ORGANIZATIONS

If you are writing a Tennessee church history, you might be interested in knowing that church-affiliated organizations exist that may be able to help with your research. Major denominational historical facilities can be located in the *Directory of Historical Organizations in the United States and Canada*, Fourteenth Edition, edited by Mary Bray Wheeler, and published in 1990 by the American Association for State and Local History in Nashville. Several of these organizations are domiciled in Tennessee. They are:

TENNESSEE BAPTIST HISTORICAL SOCIETY
P. O. Box 347
Brentwood, Tennessee 37027
(615) 373-2255

HISTORICAL FOUNDATION OF THE CUMBERLAND PRESBYTERIAN CHURCH
1978 Union Street
Memphis, Tennessee 38104
(901) 276-8602

JEWISH HISTORICAL SOCIETY OF MEMPHIS
163 Beale Street
Memphis, Tennessee 38103
(901) 682-3023

ARCHIVES OF THE JEWISH FEDERATION OF NASHVILLE AND MIDDLE TENNESSEE
801 Percy Warner Boulevard
Nashville, Tennessee 37205
(615) 356-7170

DISCIPLES OF CHRIST HISTORICAL SOCIETY
1101 19th Avenue, South
Nashville, Tennessee 37212
(615) 327-1444

GOSPEL ADVOCATE ARCHIVES AND LIBRARY
1006 Elm Hill Pike
Nashville, Tennessee 37210
(615) 254-8781

SOUTHERN BAPTIST CONVENTION AND SOUTHERN BAPTIST HISTORICAL LIBRARY AND ARCHIVES
901 Commerce Street, Suite 400
Nashville, Tennessee 37203
(615) 244-0344

UNITED METHODIST PUBLISHING HOUSE LIBRARY
201 Eighth Avenue, South
Nashville, Tennessee 37202
(615) 749-6437

WHAT ARE THE KEYS TO GOOD RESEARCH AND WRITING? 6

S o far, we've focused on the preliminaries; now we get into the real work—the research and writing. We hope the following will help you avoid some of the common pitfalls.

The previous chapters provided some suggestions for how to get started on the task of looking for sources, both published and unpublished. As you look for useful material, be open to different possibilities, including not only books, documents, and manuscript collections but also interviews, photographs, buildings, and other nontraditional forms of documentation. What is critical in every case is that you carefully determine the context in which the source was created and assess its reliability. Ask yourself the following questions:

✔ Was the source created contemporary with the event by a participant or witness?

✔ Or is it a recollection that reflects the passage of time?

✔ Is it a second-hand account, by someone who was not there?

✔ Is it the product of scholarly research?

✔ Was the source produced with some purpose in mind? Why was it created? Does that mean it may be biased? Is it reliable?

The point is not to determine whether a particular source is "good" or "bad." If used properly, a biased recollection might prove as valuable as an objective contemporary view. The point is that you have to be conscious of the context in which it was created— you must be an informed consumer of the information you use.

We assume you probably know how to take notes, but here are a few tips we've found useful:

✔ Decide on a uniform way of taking notes and stick to it—note cards, slips of paper, a laptop computer, or whatever. Believe us, its much easier to keep your project in order if you do not have to deal with bits and pieces of paper and notes in various places and in various forms.

✔ Before you start taking notes on a source, write down all the publication information you will need for citing the source. Nothing is more frustrating than having to go back to the library later to track down that information for footnotes or a bibliography.

✔ As you take notes, make sure that the source is clearly indicated on *every* notecard or slip of paper—information is useless if you do not know where it came from.

What Are the Keys to Good Research and Writing?

✔ Stick to the one-fact-to-a-card (or paper) approach—it gets tedious at times, but it is invaluable when it comes time to sort your notes and organize for writing.

✔ Remember that note taking is not just a clerical task. Do not just write down everything—try to digest the information and put it in your own words. While photocopying may ensure accuracy, it will not save time in the end—you will still have to assimilate the material before you can use it.

✔ Make sure to set off in quotation marks any language or phrases that are not your own.

✔ Code your notes to correspond to different aspects of your topic. If you tag each note with a one– or two–word description (such as, "settlement," "first election," etc.), then you will find it much easier to sort out and organize your research.

As soon as you begin a project you also begin the most important part of research—the analysis. What we mean by analysis is simply asking, "What does this information mean?" In analyzing the information you have assembled, you are trying to understand the past as more than just an accumulation of names and events. However, that is easier said than done. Perhaps the most common stumbling block is trying to determine "the truth" or "the cause." This is dangerous territory, but it is also an essential part of analysis. What you need to look for is decisive evidence—that which confirms your understanding or interpretation of the facts and denies its rival. The goal is not just consistency or plausibility, but probability. The safest ground, of course, is to look for antecedent conditions rather than "the one cause." Remember, association and causation are not the same thing. Just because two related events occurred sequentially does not mean that the first caused the second; there may be a strong association but it is not necessarily causative. Failure to recognize such distinctions can ruin a research project.

Other downfalls include:

Over–generalization—assuming what is true for the individual is true for the group.

The reductive fallacy—assuming what is true for the group applies to the individual.

Misplaced literalism—the failure to view sources in context and understand their purpose.

For further discussion of these and other historical fallacies, see David Hackett Fisher's *Historians' Fallacies: Toward a Logic of Historical Thought* (1970).

Because we like to compartmentalize and categorize, periodization also plays a role in our analysis. We have a tendency to opt for the familiar old benchmarks—wars, presidential elections, and the like—but these events or developments probably did not alter lives as much as we think. The point is that you should be open to a different timeline than what you learned in school. Do not, for example, assume that the Civil War was necessarily a turning point in the history that you are researching. If you look at a nineteenth–century industry, you may be surprised to find that the most significant developments had to do with developments other than the war. In other words, try to be open and not become boxed in by assumptions that may not be true.

The caveat about periodization is not meant to suggest that chronology is not important. Time is an essential element of history, but it should be used for more than just locating or identifying an event. Rather than just establishing when something happened, shift your focus to the passage of time—how that event or development fit into the larger process of change over time as the past became the present. This may seem like an obvious point, but too often we cannot see the forest for the chronological trees. Remember that change does not necessarily mean progress and that history has little to do with inevitability. One of the most common mistakes, for example, is to try to portray all colonial tensions or disruptions as leading inevitably to the American Revolution; colonial era history involved more than just the differences between England and its colonies and such a perspective obscures the complexity of the period.

Then there is the ultimate problem of analysis—synthesis. How do you pull it all together? There are no easy answers. The best goal is simply to strive for as reliable, honest, and logical view of the past as you can muster. You should not be afraid to admit to loose ends. But you should have as your goal understanding the past better today than you did yesterday.

For further reading on aspects of research and analysis, consider the following. This list is by no means exhaustive but should provide a good starting point.

Allen, Barbara and William Lynwood Montell. *From Memory to History Using Oral Sources in Local Historical Research.* Nashville: AASLH, 1981.

Davidson, James West and Mark Hamilton Lytle. *After the Fact: The Art of Historical Detection.* New York: Alfred A. Knopf, Inc., 1982.

Frisch, Michael. *A Shared Authority: Essays on the Craft and Meaning of Oral and Public History.* Albany: State University of New York Press, 1990.

Kyvig, David E. and Myron A. Marty. *Nearby History: Exploring the Past Around You.* Nashville: AASLH, 1982.

Ritchie, Donald A. *Doing Oral History.* New York: Twayne Publishers, 1995.

Winks, Robin W., ed. *The Historian as Detective: Essays on Evidence.* New York: Harper and Row, 1969.

How Do You Pull It All Together?

Ranking up there in its importance right beside accuracy of research and your skill at writing is the ability to produce a clean, nice-looking, readable manuscript. Having served as editors of magazines, books, newsletters, and other publications, the present authors have seen just about every kind of manuscript submission that one can think of. In general—probably due to the advent of sophisticated word processors and personal computers—the quality of manuscripts submitted by first-time authors and those who are new to the writing game has dramatically improved over the years. Unfortunately, only one word can adequately describe others: atrocious.

It is extremely difficult to understand why one would go to the trouble of spending years of his or her life researching a subject, more months, and maybe even years, to analyze and write up their findings in preparation for publication, and then devote such a small amount of time to making sure the manuscript is readable to the people who will be responsible for converting it into a marketable product. But that is exactly what happens in many instances, so we're going to take a little time to take you down the path of proper manuscript preparation. If you've already heard this lecture, you may want to simply refresh yourself with some of the main points. Here goes.

The manuscript that you send into a publishing house, regardless of whether you have a traditional publisher or are self-publishing your own book, is much like sending that publisher a large piece of your personality. From that typewritten or printed stack of paper, an astute editor draws a mental picture of whom he or she is dealing with. The old adage, "First impressions make lasting impressions," was never more true than it is in the critical step of manuscript submission.

Whether you admit it or not, you're trying to impress the editor with your ability to write. If your manuscript fails to clearly demonstrate to that editor that you have the ability to present written words in a manner that is understandable, then his or her initial impression of your skills is going to be far less than what you want it to be. Maybe the best way to explain this is to use the following example.

We're editors; you are the writer. We've talked on the phone for the past few months; maybe we've even met a time or two. We've exchanged correspondence off and on. Then the big day arrives when we've agreed that we will receive your manuscript and begin the sometimes-lengthy, complex process that will culminate with a good-looking book in your hands. We open the package and suddenly realize our worst fears.

During the course of our past written and oral communications, we've been looking forward to receiving this particular manuscript because you have made it sound so interesting and potentially salable. Now, as we gaze upon a stack of single-spaced, pale-lettered pages, with margins running to the very edges of the paper, our only thought is, "Couldn't he (or she) afford enough paper to properly express himself?" Somewhere you've lost sight (or, in your defense, maybe you never knew) what we've got to do with that glob of paper to get it into print. We'll break here a moment and tell you.

First of all—and as important an item as we'll perform—we've got to read the manuscript. A quick glance at the mass of paper on our desk tells us we've already bombed out on that one because, rather than forking out six bucks for a new type-writer or word processor ribbon, you used the one that's about ready for its hundred-thousand-mile checkup. All that our poor, word-weary eyes can decipher are pale ink marks across the pages. Secondly, if we were able to read it, one of our most important functions is to make notes in the margins for ourselves (and for you, when we return the first edited version). But what margins? We can't squeeze an exclamation mark in the margins, much less a few words or a complete sentence. Finally, some-where along the line, if all had gone well with this copy and we could use it for setting type, we would need to issue instructions to the typesetter via mutually understandable typesetters' marks between lines, in the margin, etc. Sorry, no room for this. Where are we? Is a ream of paper so expensive that you couldn't afford to use ample margins and double space the sentences? We're frustrated.

Well, enough of the negative. You get the drift. In order to make most editors happy about the manuscript you send in and he or she is about to read and process, all you have to do is follow a few simple rules. Here goes.

1. Use white, 20-pound paper, sized 8 1/2 X 11 inches, typed or printed on one side only.

2. Always double-space your work, no ifs, ands, or buts.

3. Leave about 1 1/4 inches at the top, at the bottom, and on the sides of the page to allow the editor room to make remarks.

4. Number the pages sequentially. You need not worry at this point that the table of contents, preface, list of illustrations, and other front matter will most likely carry Roman numerals in the book. Just start on the first page with 1.

5. Preface your manuscripts (whether they be for books or for magazine articles) with a page (page 1) setting forth in the middle your full name, address, telephone and FAX numbers, and social security number.

6. Make a copy of the printed manuscript to keep in a safe place. If you produced your book on a word processor or a personal computer, back up the disk(s) and keep them in two separate places in case of fire, etc.

7. Don't staple anything, and don't punch holes in the manuscript for a loose-leaf binder. Simply use one of those huge metal clips to hold the pages together.

8. Wrap the manuscript between two pieces of stiff cardboard, put a couple of rubber bands around the package, place it in a properly addressed, sufficiently sized envelope, and mail it first class or priority mail. If your editor is expecting the manuscript, and if his or her organization is a large one with many levels of assistant editors, clerks, etc., simply print "Requested Material" in large letters on the outside of the envelope. That way, your package won't get hijacked in the mail room or diverted to a generic editor.

9. Your publisher may also want the manuscript on a disk (converted to some popular personal computer word processing language like WordPerfect or Microsoft Word)—this is becoming increasingly popular, to the extent that many publishers demand a disk. To send a disk to your publisher, carefully wrap it (rigid, cardboard disk mailers are available at office supply stores) and mail it in the same package as you mail the manuscript. Be sure to send along the names of your disk files so the person at the other end will have no difficulty bringing up your files on his or her PC.

And don't forget illustrations! The old adage that a picture is worth a thousand words seems to be particularly true when it comes to writing history. That artist who diligently worked at his paints two hundred years ago, or that photographer trying out his brand new equipment at the turn of the century saw things with their eyes that are no longer present for current generations to behold. Thanks to these

Sample photo—the old Franklin interurban trolley. *Photo courtesy of Rosalie Batson.*

archivists of yesteryear, many of the lost sites, people from the past, and other objects of value have been captured forever in some form of art, whether it be paintings, maps, engravings, or photographs. By all means, if you are lucky enough to turn up one or more of these renditions in your research, consider using them in your book. When carefully chosen, they can enhance your efforts to verbalize how things once were.

Including illustrations will, however, add to the cost of publishing your book. The cheapest to repro-duce is what is called line art—basically artwork such as a pen–and–ink drawing that contains no shadows. Reproducing photographs and paintings involves a more complicated and expensive process, and color photography or other color art work is much more expensive than black and white. If at all possible, stick with something that can be reproduced in your book in black and white. Of, course, this does not preclude your having made a black-and-white image for publication purposes from a color photo.

If you locate suitable illustrative material in a private collection, you should borrow the original only long enough to take it to a private photography studio in your hometown or somewhere close to have it reproduced. The cost is nominal, and you can breath a sigh of relief when you are no longer responsible for the safety of what may be a family heirloom. And, don't forget to acknowledge the source of the illustration. In most cases, a simple statement under the caption will do, something like "Photograph courtesy of Mrs. John Smith," or "Taken from an original photograph courtesy of Mrs. John Smith," or something to that effect. If the illustration comes from the collections of a library, museum, or other institution, they may require specific language in the caption. The point is, publicly thank the person or institution from whence the illustration came.

If you intend using a photo, map, or engraving from a published book, don't forget the illustrations in that book are governed by the same copyright law that protects the text (*see* chap. 8 for a discussion on copyright law). You usually need written permission from the institution or person who owns the original illustration, map, etc. in order to use it.

Keep in mind that, when a photo is printed in a book or newspaper, it has to undergo a process called "screening." This simply means that a fine screen is used over the photograph, breaking it into thousands of tiny dots, so that when it is ready to print, the ink has something to adhere to. Use a strong magnifying glass and look at a photo in your newspaper—you can clearly see the dots. When an already screened photo is re-photographed, the camera picks up all those dots whether you see them or not. Then, when the re-shot photo is screened again, a strange-looking pattern is produced that is unacceptable for reproduction. The point is, it is extremely difficult to photograph an existing printed photograph (from a book for instance) and expect to get decent quality. It is always best, if at all possible, to supply the publisher with a glossy photo made from an original.

If you deem it absolutely necessary to illustrate your book but your research turns up no relevant photos or other art work, you may consider hiring an artist to draw or paint original material. Of course, this can get expensive, and that final decision to illustrate or not rests with you and your budget. There is also the possibility that contemporary photos will work for your book. If so, and if you do the photography yourself, buy a decent 35mm camera and use good quality black and white film.

Pretty simple, huh? You bet it's simple, and most of the procedure involves using just plain common sense if you only stop and think about it. Nothing mysterious, nothing magical; just plain, old-fashioned common sense.

WHAT DO YOU NEED TO KNOW ABOUT COPYRIGHT?

8

In the opinion of the authors, the amount of in-depth knowledge a writer or potential writer requires about copyrights in order to get on with his work can be compared to the old Brylcreem hair dressing commercial of the 1950s—"A little dab'll do ya!" Since United States copyright law was dramatically changed in 1978 and further complicated by court cases and legislative alterations and additions, scores of books that attempt to explain the law to laymen have been written. Practically every library in the country is sure to have at least one book that satisfactorily covers the new laws and their ramifications for writers. The problem is, after one reads the books, he or she often-times is still left with an empty feeling due to the vast complexities of the individual tenets of the laws, particularly the part that governs the material produced by others that one can use for his or her own project without risking infringement. With this in mind, let's cover the points about copyright that you really need to know and leave the rest for rainy-day reading.

The first thing to remember is that copyright law is a two-edged sword. It is in place, not only to protect you as a creator of literary material, but also to protect others from you should you have the urge to misuse someone else's work. It's as simple as that.

We'll take the easy part first. Normally, if you go to a publisher to produce your book, he will copyright it in your own name. There are exceptions, and one of the present authors has books copyrighted in his own name, while others are copyrighted in the publisher's name. If we could have our way every time, we would prefer to have the copyright in our own names every time, but we are also practical enough to bend a little if the placement of copyright is the only point standing in the way of a nice publishing contract. Since most book contracts are very similar and, if they are complete, minutely spell out who gets what in the event of just about any foreseeable eventuality, the writer is normally well protected, regardless of who owns the copyright.

The law requires that a copyright notice be printed in each and every copy of a published work in which copyright is claimed. Your publisher should handle this for you, but it will be your responsibility if you self–publish. The notice is usually printed on the reverse side of the title page. A suitable notice is simply, "Copyright 1995 by Joe Smith." While technically copyright exists from the moment a work is created, you gain added protection by registering your copyright with the Copyright Office. For the necessary forms, write to:

Register of Copyrights
Library of Congress
101 Independence Avenue, SE
Washington, D.C. 20540-4320

Complete the form as directed and send it, two copies of the book, and the fee requested (twenty dollars at the time of writing) to the Copyright Office. In several weeks, you will receive a copy of the registration certificate. Put it in a safe place, and you're in business. Generally speaking, with the copyright now in place, either in your name or in the name of the publisher, you are protected for your lifetime plus fifty years from infringement of others upon your rights as the creator and producer of the book's contents.

The other side of the copyright coin is, unfortunately, not so simple as what we've just described. If, for example, a work is in the public domain (published in the U.S. before 1906) or if it was published by an agency of the U.S. government, it is usually a safe bet that you can use as much or as little of the material as you want with little danger of adverse consequences. However, if the work is copyrighted, you need to know a couple of facts.

First of all, you should keep in mind that copyright protection extends not only to books but also to magazine articles; photographs, paintings, and other illustrations, both published and unpublished; music; audio- and videotapes; and even unpublished letters and other manuscript materials. Material that does not bear a copyright notice may still be protected under copyright law.

FORM TX
UNITED STATES COPYRIGHT OFFICE

REGISTRATION NUMBER

_____

| TX | | TXU |

EFFECTIVE DATE OF REGISTRATION

| Month | Day | Year |

DO NOT WRITE ABOVE THIS LINE. IF YOU NEED MORE SPACE, USE A SEPARATE CONTINUATION SHEET.

1

TITLE OF THIS WORK ▼

PREVIOUS OR ALTERNATIVE TITLES ▼

PUBLICATION AS A CONTRIBUTION If this work was published as a contribution to a periodical, serial, or collection, give information about the collective work in which the contribution appeared.   **Title of Collective Work ▼**

If published in a periodical or serial give: **Volume ▼**   **Number ▼**   **Issue Date ▼**   **On Pages ▼**

2

a

NAME OF AUTHOR ▼

DATES OF BIRTH AND DEATH
Year Born ▼   Year Died ▼

Was this contribution to the work a "work made for hire"?
☐ Yes
☐ No

AUTHOR'S NATIONALITY OR DOMICILE
Name of Country
OR { Citizen of ▶ _____
Domiciled in ▶ _____

WAS THIS AUTHOR'S CONTRIBUTION TO THE WORK
Anonymous? ☐ Yes ☐ No
Pseudonymous? ☐ Yes ☐ No
If the answer to either of these questions is "Yes," see detailed instructions.

NOTE

Under the law, the "author" of a "work made for hire" is generally the employer, not the employee (see instructions). For any part of this work that was "made for hire" check "Yes" in the space provided, give the employer (or other person for whom the work was prepared) as "Author" of that part, and leave the space for dates of birth and death blank.

NATURE OF AUTHORSHIP Briefly describe nature of the material created by the author in which copyright is claimed. ▼

b

NAME OF AUTHOR ▼

DATES OF BIRTH AND DEATH
Year Born ▼   Year Died ▼

Was this contribution to the work a "work made for hire"?
☐ Yes
☐ No

AUTHOR'S NATIONALITY OR DOMICILE
Name of Country
OR { Citizen of ▶ _____
Domiciled in ▶ _____

WAS THIS AUTHOR'S CONTRIBUTION TO THE WORK
Anonymous? ☐ Yes ☐ No
Pseudonymous? ☐ Yes ☐ No
If the answer to either of these questions is "Yes," see detailed instructions.

NATURE OF AUTHORSHIP Briefly describe nature of the material created by this author in which copyright is claimed. ▼

c

NAME OF AUTHOR ▼

DATES OF BIRTH AND DEATH
Year Born ▼   Year Died ▼

Was this contribution to the work a "work made for hire"?
☐ Yes
☐ No

AUTHOR'S NATIONALITY OR DOMICILE
Name of Country
OR { Citizen of ▶ _____
Domiciled in ▶ _____

WAS THIS AUTHOR'S CONTRIBUTION TO THE WORK
Anonymous? ☐ Yes ☐ No
Pseudonymous? ☐ Yes ☐ No
If the answer to either of these questions is "Yes," see detailed instructions.

NATURE OF AUTHORSHIP Briefly describe nature of the material created by this author in which copyright is claimed. ▼

3

a **YEAR IN WHICH CREATION OF THIS WORK WAS COMPLETED** This information must be given ◀ Year in all cases.

b **DATE AND NATION OF FIRST PUBLICATION OF THIS PARTICULAR WORK** Complete this information Month ▶ _____ Day ▶ _____ Year ▶ _____ ONLY if this work has been published. ◀ Nation

4

COPYRIGHT CLAIMANT(S) Name and address must be given even if the claimant is the same as the author given in space 2. ▼

TRANSFER If the claimant(s) named here in space 4 are different from the author(s) named in space 2, give a brief statement of how the claimant(s) obtained ownership of the copyright. ▼

See instructions before completing this space

APPLICATION RECEIVED
ONE DEPOSIT RECEIVED
TWO DEPOSITS RECEIVED
REMITTANCE NUMBER AND DATE

DO NOT WRITE HERE OFFICE USE ONLY

MORE ON BACK ▶ • Complete all applicable spaces (numbers 5-11) on the reverse side of this page.
• See detailed instructions.   • Sign the form at line 10.

DO NOT WRITE HERE

Page 1 of _____ pages

Copyright form—front.

DO NOT WRITE ABOVE THIS LINE. IF YOU NEED MORE SPACE, USE A SEPARATE CONTINUATION SHEET.

PREVIOUS REGISTRATION Has registration for this work, or for an earlier version of this work, already been made in the Copyright Office?
☐ Yes ☐ No If your answer is "Yes," why is another registration being sought? (Check appropriate box) ▼

☐ This is the first published edition of a work previously registered in unpublished form.

☐ This is the first application submitted by this author as copyright claimant

☐ This is a changed version of the work, as shown by space 6 on this application.

If your answer is "Yes," give: **Previous Registration Number** ▼   **Year of Registration** ▼

5

DERIVATIVE WORK OR COMPILATION Complete both space 6a & 6b for a derivative work; complete only 6b for a compilation.
a. **Preexisting Material** Identify any preexisting work or works that this work is based on or incorporates. ▼

b. **Material Added to This Work** Give a brief, general statement of the material that has been added to this work and in which copyright is claimed. ▼

See instructions before completing this space

6

—space deleted—

7

REPRODUCTION FOR USE OF BLIND OR PHYSICALLY HANDICAPPED INDIVIDUALS A signature on this form at space 10, and a check in one of the boxes here in space 8, constitutes a non-exclusive grant of permission to the Library of Congress to reproduce and distribute solely for the blind and physically handicapped and under the conditions and limitations prescribed by the regulations of the Copyright Office: (1) copies of the work identified in space 1 of this application in Braille (or similar tactile symbols); or (2) phonorecords embodying a fixation of a reading of that work; or (3) both.

a ☐ Copies and Phonorecords   b ☐ Copies Only   c ☐ Phonorecords Only

See instructions

8

DEPOSIT ACCOUNT If the registration fee is to be charged to a Deposit Account established in the Copyright Office, give name and number of Account.
Name ▼   Account Number ▼

9

CORRESPONDENCE Give name and address to which correspondence about this application should be sent. Name/Address/Apt/City/State/Zip ▼

Area Code & Telephone Number ►

Be sure to give your daytime phone number

CERTIFICATION* I, the undersigned, hereby certify that I am the
Check one ►
☐ author
☐ other copyright claimant
☐ owner of exclusive right(s)
☐ authorized agent of
Name of author or other copyright claimant, or owner of exclusive right(s) ▲

of the work identified in this application and that the statements made by me in this application are correct to the best of my knowledge.

Typed or printed name and date ▼ If this application gives a date of publication in space 3, do not sign and submit it before that date.

_____ date ►

Handwritten signature (X) ▼

10

MAIL CERTIFICATE TO

Certificate will be mailed in window envelope

Name ▼

Number/Street/Apartment Number ▼

City/State/Zip ▼

- Complete all necessary spaces
- Sign your application in space 10

1. Application form
2. Nonrefundable $20 filing fee in check or money order payable to Register of Copyrights
3. Deposit material

Register of Copyrights
Library of Congress
Washington, D.C. 20559

11

* 17 U.S.C. § 506(e): Any person who knowingly makes a false representation of a material fact in the application for copyright registration provided for by section 409, or in any written statement filed in connection with the application, shall be fined not more than $2,500.

February 1991—200,000   ☆U.S. GOVERNMENT PRINTING OFFICE: 1991—282-170/20,010

Copyright form—back.

Second, under the "fair use" principle embedded in current copyright law, one is allowed to quote copyrighted material of others without fear of infringement up to a certain point, but just what that point is was purposely not defined in the copyright revisions of the past several years. Is a paragraph too much, or a page, or two pages, or what? Obviously, one should not pick up the work of another and simply reproduce page after page of material, but what if you want to use a single paragraph that someone else has written that so succinctly explains your point that it seems useless trying to phrase it differently? In the first chapter of this book, we quoted from a book by David E. Kyvig and Myron A. Marty. To us, this is a classic example of fair use. We did not obtain permission to use the quotation, because in no way did our use of this small piece of Kyvig and Marty's book detract from it, distort it, or jeopardize sales of it.

Ideally, to be on the safe side every time, one should write and obtain permission for every direct quotation that you intend to use in your book. Believe us, this can be extremely tedious and sparsely rewarding, particularly since half of the time the authors or publishers from whom you are requesting the permission will fail to respond anyway. Also, requesting permission could lead to trouble—if the copyright owner wants to be difficult, he or she could interpret your request as an admission that the use exceeds what is fair. Probably a good rule of thumb would be to discuss any quoted material with your publisher and decide together whether special permission should be obtained. On the other hand, don't forget that most contracts contain a specific article that holds the publisher harmless in lawsuits involving infringement, so that in reality, the decision to obtain permission or to forego it eventually falls back on you, the writer. Of course, if you are going the self-publishing route, the entire decision is yours.

Regardless of whether or not you deem it necessary to obtain permission from a writer or a publisher to use information or directly quote from his or her property, you must give credit in your book to the source of the quotation or the utilized data. This should be done with a footnote, endnote, or other method of documentation. For examples of four different methods, see the section on documentation in *The Chicago Manual of Style*, the guide used by most publishers on such matters. While a publisher may not like any of the methods and may try to talk you out of formal citation of your sources, you should insist on proper attribution—you are obligated, both legally and ethically, to provide such information.

Not providing an appropriate citation constitutes plagiarism—the expropriation of another's text and the presentation of it as your own. The issue is not length or other factors that come into play with the fair use principle, but rather appropriate attribution when you use someone else's words or text. Regardless of whether a passage or text is brief enough to fall under the fair use category, the original author must be given credit. Even when you paraphrase another's work, there is potential for misuse—too many paraphrases linked together demonstrate dependence on another's work that also must be acknowledged. The best prevention is to develop careful work habits, always making clear in your notes when you are quoting or closely para-phrasing another author and always taking care to give credit where credit is due.

If you feel that you need more information on copyright, find a good, recently published book on the subject, such as *The Copyright Book: A Practical Guide*, by William S. Strong, published in 1990 by the MIT Press of Cambridge, Massachusetts.

WHERE CAN YOU FIND A PUBLISHER?

9

At some point in your writing career, you must make a decision about how you intend to get your book into print. In the ideal world, you will have already found a publisher for your project, hammered out the details of a contract, and signed the document before you even start to write the manuscript. In this manner—upon completing the research and writing phases—you simply turn your typewritten or printed pages over to the publisher, wait a few months for the book to be edited, typeset, and manufactured, and one day, open the mail to find several copies of your book, beautifully printed and bound with a message that the remainder of the copies have been nationally distributed. Then, about six months later, the royalties start flooding in and you look for ways to invest the obscene amount of money that you begin to receive for your years of hard work. Not!

Unfortunately, life in the real world of writing and publishing does not work exactly like the above scenario. Until about a decade ago, a small, but dedicated, group of book publishers enthusiastically supported quality local and regional history. Sadly, however, during the late 1980s and early 1990s, this healthy picture began to change. With the advent of business takeovers and mergers, corporate raiders, increased expenses, and absolute no-nonsense bottom lines on profit and loss statements, publishers who were willing to take the financial risks involved in producing and marketing books designed primarily for a limited, localized audience became increasingly rare.

Of course, this "I'm not interested in your manuscript unless I (the publisher) can make lots of money on it" attitude has tremendous implications for us as writers. It means that our book proposal has become just another commodity in the everyday marketplace of American commerce, nothing more, nothing less. Our carefully laid out plans for researching and writing a book about a local event or person that has never before been told now falls into the same category as hog bellies and wheat futures on the altar of profitability. It matters not that our book will fill a vacuum in the literature of the region, or that it is well-crafted and beautifully written, or that it contributes much-needed information to the complex story of Tennessee and its business, religious, or educational institutions. None of these elements matter because, whether you like it or not, most American publishers' primary and overriding consideration in reaching a decision to publish or not to publish your book is, quite simply, its marketability, i.e., its potential sales.

After having said all this, let's talk about alternatives to the traditional writer-publisher relationship.

Where Can You Find a Publisher?

Let's talk about a process that for years was considered so taboo among literary critics that most writers' organizations refused to consider for membership an author guilty of having his or her book so published. Let's talk about a process that disallowed its participants to enter their books, regardless of how noteworthy or superbly written, into literary competition. Let's talk about self-publishing.

So that there will be *absolutely no surprises* at the end of this discussion, particularly to newcomers to the writing and publishing fields, all self-publishing programs are synonymous with self-funded programs. We'll say it a different way: quite simply, the writer or a financial backer pays for the project. But, there is far more that you need to know about self-publishing than who is going to pay the tariff. Please read on.

For years we have read the thinly disguised advertisements for so-called "vanity" publishers, most of them located in New York City. These are the guys who produce the glitzy brochures about how wonderful they are, take your money, quickly "publish" your book—oftentimes without even making an effort to edit it—and send back however many copies of an ill-designed and shabbily produced book that your hard-earned money will pay for. It's as simple as that— no editorial expertise, no marketing assistance, no distribution advice, no nothing, except the books.

Then, there is the local quick-print method of publishing, which is nothing more than contract printing. You simply carry your stuff in to the corner print shop, tell them how many copies you want, and pay them. Genealogists have been going this route for

years, and regardless of how much wonderful information and data some of these labors of love contain,
they surely rank among some of the ugliest, unpro-
fessional-looking volumes ever produced by mankind.

In either of the above two scenarios, please note
that you, the writer, have also assumed the mantle of
chief editor, designer, marketing representative, sales
associate, and delivery person. Quite frankly, neither
of us has any business attempting to fill any of these
jobs. We are researchers and writers, and researchers
and writers we should continue to be.

Fortunately for all of us, another breed of book-
publishing professional has arrived upon the
American scene in recent years. In many instances,
these new outfits, which, for lack of a better term
we'll call self-publishing consultants and packagers,
are owned and managed by former executives in the
traditional publishing world who recognized early on
in their careers that an essential need existed for
people like us who had valid, worthwhile stories to
tell, but whose ideas were regionally or locally
oriented, and thus, from a purely commercial and
marketing standpoint, limited in appeal.

The bottom-line, good news about this interesting
concept in self-publishing is quite exciting. In more
cases than not, for the same price or less, the author
receives for his money a professionally copy edited,
uniquely designed, and professionally produced book
that can proudly stand among the best-looking
volumes on anybody's bookshelf. And, for you the
author—although your book might have limited
appeal for readers in only a tiny sector of the state or
region—some of these same self-publishers already

have relationships with national book distributors and some have become so successful at what they do that they produce their own exclusive catalog of the works they have produced for hire!

Don't let this last thought get lost in the shuffle. Think about it. Your book, which you originally thought would be of interest only to residents of Wazoo County, now, by virtue of its inclusion in a national book distributorship program and its presence in the publisher's exclusive catalog, can be available to former residents of Wazoo County who now live in Maine, Florida, or California. Your degree of involvement becomes as small or as large as you want it to be. Now, instead of the UPS man driving up to your house one day with a truckload of books that suddenly you realize won't even fit in your over-stuffed basement, the books go to the publisher's warehouse, where orders can be filled promptly.

The last of the three self-publishing options is obviously the one that we feel gives the prospective writer the best mileage for the money invested. And, procedurally, the entire affair is quite simple and painless. After you find such a publisher, you provide it with the specifications of your book: number of manuscript pages, number of photos and other illustrations, if any complex graphs or charts will be included, your perception of how the book should look, and other information that quite obviously figures into the cost of manufacture.

This initial step is quickly consummated by the completion of a ready-made check-list that covers all of the critical points. The publisher then prepares a custom-made proposal for your book and presents it to you. All costs, financial terms, design elements, final specifications, and distribution arrangements are spelled out therein. Upon acceptance of the contract by both parties, you, the author, will be expected to provide the publisher with a down-payment (usually one-third of the total price of the project) at contract signing, one-third at the publisher's acceptance of the final page proofs, and the final one-third when manufactured books are delivered. It's as simple as that.

In summary, the days of having purely local and regional histories published at someone else's expense are just about gone forever. The fragile position of small- and medium-sized businesses in today's economy, the expense of producing short (low volume) print runs, and the logistics of distributing books of local appeal within a national scheme of things have definitely placed a few nails at strategic places in the coffin-lid of regional publishing in America. Yet, unfortunate as that is, new and challenging ways are now available that can alleviate most of the problems of getting your book into print in a handsome format and in the quantity that you desire, and most importantly, within a financial framework that will fit your budget.

Appendix I
A Chronological
History of Tennessee

Although the documentation of local historical events provide the stepping stones for more comprehensive state, regional, and national histories, it seems to us that an understanding and appreciation of Tennessee's vast, important history is, nevertheless, in itself, essential to those wishing to study and produce such local histories. It is also obvious to us that it would be difficult, indeed, to tell Tennessee's complete story in the few pages that we have allotted for it in this book.

In order to bridge this gap, as well as to provide background information on Tennessee's history for the newcomer to the state, we have decided to provide the state's history in abbreviated form by way of the relatively comprehensive chronology given below. We are fully aware that many events that could have been covered here are not, but we believe that the chronology can be a useful tool for local historians to provide reference points to connect particular events found in their research with other events making history across the state as a whole at the same place in time. Additionally, by the very fact that it is organized in date order, a chronology provides a quicker and simpler way to ferret out desired information than wading through paragraph after paragraph of text. With this thought in mind, we present this chronology of Tennessee history.

Ca. 20–30,000 B.C.—Paleolithic Indians first populate the region of present–day Tennessee.

Ca. 6,000 B.C.—Archaic Indians move into the region and build villages.

Ca. 500–1,000 B.C.—Woodland Indians establish agriculture in the region.

Ca. 1000—Early Mississippian Indians occupy the Mississippi Valley, constructing their distinctive temple mounds.

Ca. 1300—Creek and Yuchi Indians begin erecting villages in present–day East Tennessee, and the Shawnee occupy parts of Middle Tennessee.

1540—Hernando de Soto is the first European to enter the territory that is now Tennessee.

1566–1567—Spanish explorer Juan Pardo builds a fort at the Creek town of Chiaha but soon abandons it.

1673—James Needham and Gabriel Arthur become the first Englishmen to enter Tennessee. French explorers Marquette and Joliet stop at Chickasaw Bluffs (Memphis) on their exploration of the Mississippi River.

1682—The French explorer La Salle builds Fort Prudhomme on the first Chickasaw Bluff near the mouth of the Hatchie River.

Appendix I.: A Chronological History of Tennessee

1692—Martin Chartier, one of La Salle's men, marries a Shawnee Indian and settles along the Cumberland River near the French Lick (Nashville).

1710—Jean de Charleville, a French trader, establishes a trading post at the French Lick.

1711—Eleazer Wiggan, an English trader, establishes the first European trade with the Overhill Cherokees in today's East Tennessee.

1714—Cherokee and Chickasaw Indians drive the Creek, Yuchi, and Shawnee out of Tennessee.

1730—Sir Alexander Cuming negotiates the first treaty between English authorities and Cherokee Indians.

1739—French explorers build Fort Assumption on the site of today's city of Memphis.

1750—Thomas Walker, a Virginia physician, explores upper East Tennessee, and discovers and passes through Cumberland Gap into Kentucky. He provides the names for the Cumberland River and the Cumberland Mountains.

1757—Fort Loudoun, the first British fort west of the Appalachian Mountains, is completed near the Cherokee capital of Chota, at the mouth of the Tellico River.

1758—Stephen Holston, a Virginian, travels to Tennessee and lends his name to the Holston River. Colonel Bird builds Fort Long Island on the Holston River.

1760—As conflict with their former English allies escalates, the Cherokees take Fort Loudoun. Warfare ends with the negotiation of a treaty in 1761.

71

1761—Elisha Walden and a party of long hunters explore much of East Tennessee and the Cumberland River valley.

1763—With the signing of the Treaty of Paris, France surrenders to Great Britain all claims of sovereignty over the vast region lying east of the Mississippi River.

1766—Colonel James Smith leads an exploring party into today's Middle Tennessee and discovers Stones River, named for Uriah Stone, one of the explorers in the group.

1768—Great Britain and the Cherokees sign the Treaty of Hard Labor in South Carolina, freeing much Indian land in present-day Tennessee to potential white settlement.

1769—William Bean, credited with being Tennessee's first permanent white resident, settles on Boone's Creek, near its confluence with the Watauga River.

1771—White settlers in two areas in East Tennessee—the Watauga valley close to the site of Elizabethton and the Nolichucky River valley—form the Watauga Association, the first effort at establishing organized government in the Tennessee region.

1775—North Carolina entrepreneur Richard Henderson buys millions of acres of Cherokee land situated between the Kentucky and the Cumberland Rivers.

1776–1777—War breaks out between the Cherokees and the white settlers in East Tennessee, ending with the Treaty of Long Island, giving Virginia and North Carolina control over disputed territory.

1777—The North Carolina legislature establishes Washington County, covering much of today's Tennessee.

1779—North Carolina authorities establish Jonesborough, the first town organized in Tennessee. James Robertson and his overland party reach the French Lick, the site of Nashville.

1780—John Donelson and his river party reach the French Lick settlement, which is named Fort Nashborough. The settlers sign the Cumberland Compact and organize a temporary government. Tennessee troops participate in the Battle of Kings Mountain.

1781—The Battle of the Bluffs is fought between Fort Nashborough settlers and Indians.

1783—The Cumberland settlements are organized into Davidson County, North Carolina. North Carolina grants a charter for Martin Academy in present-day East Tennessee, the first institution of higher learning in the Mississippi River valley.

1784—The State of Franklin is established and a constitution is adopted. Nashborough is incorporated and renamed Nashville.

1785—The first Franklin legislature meets at Greeneville; John Sevier is elected governor; four new counties are established.

1786—Captain James White settles present-day Knoxville.

1787—The Franklin legislature meets at Greeneville for the last time.

1788—The State of Franklin collapses. Bishop Francis Asbury holds the first Methodist Conference west of the Alleghenies.

1790—Congress passes an act to create the Territory of the United States South of the River Ohio, known as

73

the Southwest Territory. The territory covers today's state of Tennessee. William Blount is appointed territorial governor.

1792—Governor William Blount establishes the territory's capital at White's Fort (Knoxville). The *Knoxville Gazette*, a weekly published at Rogersville, becomes the first newspaper produced in the region that is soon to become Tennessee.

1793—Elections for the first territorial legislature are held. After years of conflict and war, the Cherokees are forced to concede white control over disputed lands.

1794—The first territorial legislature meets at Knoxville. Blount College, forerunner to the University of Tennessee, is chartered.

1795—Walton Road is completed from Kingston to Nashville across the Cumberland Plateau.

1796—The first Tennessee state constitution is adopted. Tennessee County is divided into two entities and renamed Robertson and Montgomery Counties, so that the name "Tennessee" can be given to the state. Tennessee's first general assembly meets at Knoxville. John Sevier becomes Tennessee's first governor, William Blount and William Cocke the first U.S. senators, and Andrew Jackson the first U.S. representative. Tennessee is admitted to the Union as the sixteenth state on June 1.

1797—The *Tennessee Gazette* is established as Nashville's first newspaper. Fort Pickering is built on the site of Memphis.

1800—Congress designates the Natchez Trace as the official post road between Nashville and Natchez.

Appendix I.: A Chronological History of Tennessee

1804—The Tennessee legislature passes a law to regulate the construction of public roads.

1807—The Bank of Nashville, the first financial institution in Tennessee, is chartered.

1810—The Cumberland Presbyterian Church is organized in Dickson County.

1811—Reelfoot Lake is created by a devastating series of earthquakes.

1812—The Tennessee legislature meets in Nashville for the first time.

1814—Andrew Jackson defeats the Creek Indians at the Battle of Horseshoe Bend, ending the Creek War.

1815—General Andrew Jackson's army of Tennesseans, Kentuckians, blacks, and pirates defeats British forces at New Orleans.

1817—Knoxville becomes the state capital again.

1818—The state capital moves to Murfreesboro. West Tennessee is acquired as part of the Jackson Purchase.

1819—The first steamboat on the Cumberland River, the *General Jackson*, arrives at Nashville. John Overton lays out the city of Memphis. At Jonesborough, Elihu Embree publishes the *Manumission Intelligencer*, later called the *Emancipator*, the first anti-slavery newspaper in the United States.

1820—Andrew Jackson's military road connecting Nashville and Madisonville, Louisiana, is completed.

1823—The *Pioneer*, the first newspaper in West Tennessee, is published at Jackson. The first public school law in the state is enacted.

1826—The capital returns to Nashville. Cumberland College, formerly Davidson Academy, becomes the University of Nashville.

1826—The Memphis *Advocate*, first newspaper in Memphis, is published.

1828—Andrew Jackson defeats John Quincy Adams for the presidency of the United States. Knoxville receives its first visit from a steamboat, the *Atlas*.

1831—The first macadamized road in the state is built.

1832—Andrew Jackson is re-elected to his second term as president.

1833—A severe epidemic of Asiatic cholera sweeps over Tennessee.

1834—A new state constitution is adopted by convention.

1838—Removal of Cherokees from Tennessee to lands west of the Mississippi begins.

1839—The town of Chattanooga is established on the banks of the Tennessee River near the homeplace of Cherokee leader John Ross.

1842—The first train ever to run in Tennessee makes an exhibition run over the LaGrange and Memphis railroad.

1843—The state legislature designates Nashville as Tennessee's permanent capital.

1844—Tennessean James K. Polk, the first "dark horse" presidential candidate in U.S. history, is elected to the presidency.

Appendix I.: A Chronological History of Tennessee

1845—Work begins on the capitol building in Nashville. Andrew Jackson dies at the Hermitage.

1846—War with Mexico is declared by President Polk. Before the conflict is over, thirty thousand Tennesseans will volunteer their services to the military, reaffirming Tennessee's reputation as the "Volunteer" state.

1849—Former President James K. Polk dies in Nashville.

1850—Representatives of slave–holding states convene the Southern Convention, holding a nine-day session in Nashville to discuss the slavery issue.

1853—The Tennessee legislature meets in the new capitol building for the first time.

1855—The capitol building is completed.

1860—The Constitutional Union Party opens its convention in Baltimore and nominates Nashvillian John Bell as its presidential candidate. Bell is later defeated by Abraham Lincoln.

1861—Governor Isham Harris proclaims Tennessee's secession from the Union on June 24.

1862—Confederate Forts Henry and Donelson surrender to Union forces; the latter occupy Nashville in late February. The Battle of Shiloh is fought on April 6 and 7. Memphis surrenders to Union troops on June 6. The Army of Tennessee fails to recapture Middle Tennessee.

1863—Knoxville falls to the Union on August 24. The Confederate army defeats Union troops at the Battle of Chickamauga on September 19–20, but in November Union forces rout the Confederates at the Battle of Chattanooga.

1864—Tennessee's military governor, Andrew Johnson, is elected vice-president of the U.S. on November 4. Confederate and Union troops clash at Franklin on November 30. December 15–16, Confederates lose the Battle of Nashville, the last significant battle in the war.

1865—Andrew Johnson becomes president following the assassination of President Abraham Lincoln. Tennessee ratifies the Thirteenth Amendment.

1866—Tennessee becomes the first former Confederate state to re-enter the Union. The forerunner of Fisk University, a school for freed slaves, opens in Nashville.

1870—The Constitution of 1870, Tennessee's third such instrument, is adopted; it gives all male citizens age twenty-one and older the right to vote. Randall Brown is elected one of three Davidson County commissioners, thus becoming the first black man to hold an elective office in the state.

1872—Vanderbilt University is established in Nashville.

1875—Former President Andrew Johnson dies near Jonesborough.

1876—Meharry Medical College is founded as part of Central Tennessee College.

1878—One of the worst yellow fever epidemics in U.S. history visits Memphis, killing about five thousand of the city's 19,600 residents.

1879—The Memphis city charter is revoked by the state legislature because of the yellow fever epidemic.

1882—Julia Doak is appointed state superintendent of education, the first woman in American history to hold such an office.

Appendix I.: A Chronological History of Tennessee

1887—The Tennessee National Guard is organized. A prohibition amendment to the state constitution is defeated by popular vote.

1890—The Chickamauga-Chattanooga National Military Park is established.

1897—The Tennessee Centennial Exposition opens in Nashville one year late.

1898—The gunboat *Nashville* fires the first shot in the Spanish-American War.

1905—The Tennessee state flag is adopted on April 17.

1906—Overton Park Zoo is established at Memphis.

1907—Purchase of a Governor's Mansion, located on Seventh Avenue one-half block south of the Capitol, is authorized.

1909—State-wide prohibition law passes, to become effective on July 1.

1911—The legislature passes a child labor law.

1918—Sergeant Alvin York, a farm boy from Pall Mall, becomes the greatest hero of the great war in Europe, capturing 132 Germans singlehandedly. He is awarded a medal of honor.

1919—Hamilton and James Counties become the first county consolidation in the United States. Tennessee's women's suffrage bill is enacted.

1920—Tennessee legislators ratify the 19th Amendment (women's suffrage). The state provides the final ratification required to add the amendment to the U.S. Constitution.

1922—The first official government airmail in the South, connecting Nashville and Chicago, is inaugurated. The first commercial radio broadcasting station in Tennessee begins operations in Nashville.

1925—The first scheduled airline operation in Tennessee begins in Chattanooga. John Scopes, a Rhea County high school teacher, is convicted of teaching the theory of evolution in his classroom, in direct violation of a recently passed law prohibiting such.

1926—WSM Radio in Nashville originates the Grand Ole Opry.

1928—Four new bridges are erected over the Tennessee River.

1929—The federal government accepts an offer of land from Tennessee and North Carolina for the establishment of the Great Smoky Mountains National Park.

1933—Tennessee adopts the iris as the state flower and the mockingbird as the state bird. The U.S. Congress establishes the Tennessee Valley Authority (TVA), and construction of the system's first dam, Norris, begins.

1934—Congress establishes the Great Smoky Mountains National Park.

1935—Construction begins on modern airports for Nashville, Chattanooga, Memphis, and the Tri-city communities.

1936—Norris Dam is completed and produces its first hydroelectric power.

1943—The Grand Ole Opry selects the Ryman Auditorium in Nashville as its permanent home.

1944—The Holston Ordnance Works at Kingsport becomes the world's largest manufacturer of RDX, the most powerful explosive known before the advent of the atomic bomb.

1945—Tennessean Cordell Hull is awarded the Nobel Peace Prize. Government officials announce that the secret facilities at Oak Ridge are in reality the administrative headquarters for the atomic bomb project. Official tabulations reflect that 315,501 Tennesseans served in World War II.

1947—The Tennessee legislature enacts the first sales tax.

1949—The gates to Oak Ridge are opened to the public for the first time. Camp Forrest at Tullahoma is selected by the Army Air Force as the site of its Air Engineering Development Center (later called the Arnold Engineering Development Center) to be built in 1950.

1951—The office of lieutenant-governor is created by the legislature. Tennessee A & I College, the only tax-supported black college in the state, is elevated to university status.

1952—For the first time since 1928, a majority of Tennesseans vote Republican in the presidential election. The country's first Holiday Inn opens in Memphis.

1953—Tennessee's first constitutional convention in eighty-three years meets in Nashville. Voters adopt all eight of the constitutional amendments proposed by the convention, and the amendments become official on November 19.

1954—E. H. "Boss" Crump, Memphis political kingpin, dies.

1955—The office of state historian is created by the General Assembly with Robert H. White as the first appointee.

1956—Governor Frank Clement is the keynote speaker at the Democratic National Convention. Senator Estes Kefauver is nominated as the party's candidate for vice-president.

1957—At Clinton High School, Bobby Cain becomes the first African-American to graduate from an integrated high school in the South.

1960—Citizens of Nashville and Davidson vote to consolidate their city and county powers into one "metro" government. Tennesseans Wilma Rudolph and Ralph Boston win multiple gold medals for track at the Olympic games in Rome.

1965—A. W. Willis Jr. becomes the first African-American representative elected to the General Assembly in sixty-five years.

1966—Howard Baker is elected to the U.S. Senate, becoming only the third Republican from Tennessee to serve there.

1968—Civil rights leader Martin Luther King is assassinated in Memphis on April 4.

1970—Winfield Dunn becomes the first Republican to gain the governor's chair in fifty years.

1972—Opryland USA opens, drawing 1,400,000 people during its first year of operation.

1977—Elvis Presley dies in Memphis. Alex Haley is awarded the Pulitzer Prize for *Roots*.

1979—In an unprecedented move, the governor-elect, Lamar Alexander, is sworn into office three days early due to irregularities being investigated in Governor Ray Blanton's office. Blanton is later indicted and convicted of corruption in the allocation of state liquor licenses.

1980—Jane Eskind of Nashville becomes the first woman to win a statewide election in Tennessee, becoming a member of the Public Service Commission. Memphis attorney George Brown becomes the first African American to sit on the Tennessee Supreme Court. The Nissan Corporation of Tokyo announces plans to build the largest truck assembly plant in the world in Smyrna.

1982—The World's Fair opens in Knoxville. Lamar Alexander becomes the first person in Tennessee's history to be elected to two successive four-year terms as governor.

1986—Ned Ray McWherter is elected governor, thus returning the state's political control to the Democrats.

1987—The University of Tennessee's Lady Vols basketball team wins the NCAA National Championship. Construction is completed on General Motors' new Saturn Corporation auto plant near Spring Hill.

1992—The Democratic party regains the White House with a ticket that includes Tennessean Albert Gore Jr. as vice–president.

1993—West Tennessee born Tina Turner's life is documented in the widely received movie, *What's Love Got to Do With It?*

1994—The GOP dominates the fall elections by sending Republicans Fred Thompson and Bill Frist to the U.S. Senate and Don Sundquist to the governor's mansion. Wilma Rudolph, 1960 Olympic gold medalist from Clarksville, dies on November 12.

1995—Andrew Lytle, the last of the Vanderbilt "Agrarian" writers, dies at Monteagle on December 13 at the age of ninety-two.

1996—Tennessee celebrates its bicentennial.

APPENDIX II
TENNESSEE STATE AND
COUNTY HISTORIANS (1995)

State Historian—Mrs. Wilma Dykeman Stokely

Anderson	Ms. Sue Harris	**Hamblen**	Mrs. Berwin Haun
Bedford	Mr. Richard Poplin	**Hamilton**	Mr. John Wilson
Benton	Mrs. Virginia L. Whitworth	**Hancock**	Mr. Scott Collins
Bledsoe	Miss Elizabeth Robnett	**Hardeman**	Mrs. Faye Tennyson Davidson
Blount	Mrs. Inez Burns	**Hardin**	Ms. Mary Hitchcock
Bradley	Dr. Bill Snell	**Hawkins**	Mr. Henry R. Price
Campbell	None	**Haywood**	Ms. Lynn Shaw
Cannon	Mr. Harold Patrick		Mrs. J. C. Nunn
Carroll	Mrs. Mary Ruth Devault		Mr. Ray Dixon
Carter	None	**Henderson**	Mr. Randy Hart
Cheatham	Mr. James B. Hallums	**Henry**	Ms. Mary Ashley Morris
Chester	Mr. Bobby Barnes	**Hickman**	Mr. Edward Dotson
	Mr. Lewis Jones	**Houston**	Mr. George Bateman
	Mr. James Williams	**Humphreys**	Mrs. Bill Anderson
Claiborne	Mr. John J. Kivette		Mr. John H. Whitfield
Clay	Mrs. W. B. Upton	**Jackson**	Ms. Moldon Tayse
Cocke	Mr. Edward R. Walker III	**Jefferson**	Dr. E. P. Muncy
Coffee	Mr. Jess Lewis Jr.	**Johnson**	Mr. Thomas W. Gentry
Crockett	Mrs. Charles C. James	**Knox**	Mrs. Park Niceley
Cumberland	Mr. Donald Brookhart	**Lake**	Ms. Abigail Hyde
Davidson	Mr. John L. Connelly	**Lauderdale**	Mr. Terry Ford
Decatur	Mrs. Lillye Younger	**Lawrence**	Ms. Kathy Niedergeses
DeKalb	Mr. Thomas G. Webb	**Lewis**	Ms. Marjorie B. Graves
Dickson	Mr. George Jackson	**Lincoln**	Mrs. Sarah B. Posey
Dyer	Mr. Wallace Milan	**Loudon**	Mr. Joe Spence
Fayette	Mrs. J. R. Morton	**Macon**	Mr. Harold Blankenship
Fentress	Ms. Lorraine Cargile	**Madison**	Mr. Harbert Alexander
Franklin	Mr. Howard M. Hannah	**Marion**	Mrs. Patsy Beene
Gibson	Mr. Fred Culp	**Marshall**	Ms. Charlene Nicholas
Giles	Mrs. Pauline Cross	**Maury**	Mrs. Marise Lightfoot
Grainger	Mr. John M. Clark	**McMinn**	Mr. Bill Akins
Greene	Mr. T. Elmer Cox	**McNairy**	Mr. Bill Wagoner
Grundy	Ms. Margaret Coppinger	**Meigs**	Ms. Shirley Jennings
	Mr. William Ray Turner		Ms. Paulette Jones

Monroe	Mr. Walter Lumsden Jr.
Montgomery	Ms. Eleanor Williams
Moore	Mrs. Joyce Neal
Morgan	Mr. Donald Todd
Obion	Mr. Rebel C. Forrester
Overton	None
Perry	Mr. Gus A. Steele
Pickett	Mr. Richard W. Pierce
Polk	Ms. Marian Presswood
Putnam	Ms. Pat Franklin
Rhea	Ms. Betty Broyles
Roane	Mr. J. C. Parker
Robertson	Ms. Yolanda Reid
Rutherford	Mr. Ernest K. Johns
Scott	Ms. Irene Baker
Sequatchie	Mr. Henry Camp
Sevier	Mrs. Beulah D. Linn
Shelby	Mr. Edward F. Williams III
Smith	Mr. Ervin Smith
Stewart	Ms. Nelda Saunders
Sullivan	Dr. Elery A. Lay
Sumner	Dr. John Garrott
Tipton	Mr. Russell Bailey
Trousdale	Mr. Web Ross
Unicoi	Mr. Walter B. Garland
Union	Ms. Bonnie H. Peters
Van Buren	Mr. Earl J. Madewell
Warren	Mr. James A. Dillon Jr.
Washington	Mrs. Ruth Broyles
Wayne	Mr. Alf Scott
Weakley	Mrs. Virginia C. Vaughan
White	Ms. Mary West
Williamson	Mrs. Joe Bowman
Wilson	Mr. William Simms